Praise for *The Quest for Durability*

"A must read for growing businesses in all stages of development. This book covers a practical approach to drive business commercialization with a strategic focus on the all-important goals of creating a sustainable business lifecycle with lasting value. It's a guide to crafting an evolving roadmap for a successful and durable enterprise."

—Mario M. Casabona, Casabona Ventures and TechLaunch, Founder and Managing Director.

"The Quest for Durability tackles a key task of every business and organization leadership team, which is how to develop and implement strategic actions to grow and sustain profitable, justifiable competitive advantages. It features *The Business Puzzle Method*™, a cutting-edge methodology that recognizes and places the burden of business model validation on customer acceptance in this rapidly changing world with so many challenges and endless opportunities. If you're seeking durable business success and excellence, this book not only offers a management practice and philosophy to achieve it, but also maintain it!"

—Dr. Randall Pinkett, Chairman and CEO, BCT Partners.

"Jerry Creighton has great insight in identifying the needs and performance for continuous business growth and direction. This book charts the path and techniques for continuous growth and long-term success from the The Quest for Durability. It is a valuable tool for company success."

—Katherine O'Neill, Co-Founder Broad Street Angels, Member Jumpstart NJ Angel Network, Rowan University Investment Board.

Dedication

I dedicate this book to my mom and dad who taught me the value of hard work and perseverance based on a solid value system.

I am also truly grateful to my wife Isabel, my previous business partner and a person who is always there for me with her keen advice and supported me in the life we encountered...a life full of interesting experiences, transitions and learnings.

The Quest for Durability

—The Business Puzzle Method™

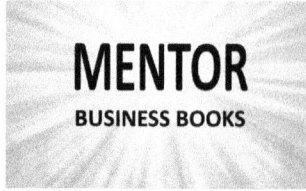

MENTOR
BUSINESS BOOKS

Manhanset House
Shelter Island Hts., New York 11965-0342

bricktower@aol.com • tech@absolutelyamazingebooks.com
• absolutelyamazingebooks.com

Library of Congress Cataloging-in-Publication Data
Creighton Sr., Jerry
The Quest For Durability—The Business Puzzle Method™
p. cm.

1. Business / Entrepreneurship. 2. Business / Methods / Procedures. 3. Business / Management. Non-Fiction, I. Title.
ISBN: 978-1-955036-48-1, Trade Paper

June 2023

The Quest for Durability

—The Business Puzzle Method™

www.JerryCreighton.com

Jerry Creighton, Sr., MBA

Habent Sua Fata Libelli

Acknowledgments

This book is the result of many years of my experiences and learnings which added to my knowledge and preparation of the business development practices covered in this book. Naming individuals from my experiences would be a real challenge because there were so many. I chose to not include individual's names to avoid arousing resentment from those who were not mentioned, with one exception. Most recently, my sincere thanks to my friend and editor Barry Cohen who helped me organize and finalize the manuscript for this book.

Yes, my preparation of the Acknowledgment page of this book is an unconventional one, but so are many of the themes behind *The Quest for Durability / The Business Puzzle Method*™. This book can help your business be relevant, resilient and durable.

Read on!

Contents

Author's Note

A New Business Development Perspective

My fundamental premise driving this book "The Quest for Durability" is:

To be a cutting-edge business, you need to have the ability to continuously grow, create value and adapt expeditiously as needed and as planned.

Let me clearly define what I mean when I refer to business development. It means Business Transformation encompassing programs of continuous growth-oriented initiatives and being adequately prepared (year-over-year) to maintain a profitable growth trajectory.

Durability is about developing and utilizing insight and capabilities in the current and in a volatile / uncertain forward-looking customer/buyer world of evolving preferences.

Being able to position your business as a JUSTIFIABLE year-over-year durable business is a valued competency demonstrated by the most successful of businesses. Their formula is not a secret...they favor continual real-time transformational thinking. Their success is based on planned change, organizational workflow design, knowledge and insight generation, creative problem-solving, culture attributes and timely, innovative business development and execution practices. More about this in later chapters.

* * *

A KEY INSIGHT—STRATEGIES THAT EFFECT LONG-TERM BUSINESS VALUE

The business community, especially in the U.S, generally operates in a world where business is done by pursuing a short-term goal of quarterly profit reporting as the driving force. This can lead to mediocrity and complacency. Contrast that with the goal of establishing *lifecycle (year-over-year) durability* as the measure of a successful business, even for startup businesses.

"The Quest for Durability," featuring *The Business Puzzle Method*™ approach, represents *The New Standard for Business Development. Foundation principles are based on building and maintaining* ***Lifecycle Durability Focused Business Models (LDFBM)*** *that add substance to your business's operations and planning process. "The Quest for Durability" presents solutions for your business to succeed and increase* ***business lifecycle longevity****. It's about creating a blueprint and path for long-term success for startups, expansion companies and mature businesses looking for additional profitable growth."*

Business development strategies (to achieve and maintain ongoing durability) is an activity that needs to be constantly updated as your business goes through various lifecycle stages (startup, expansion, mature business). Startups, expansion and mature businesses require significantly different transition programs to reach and maintain profitable growth objectives. Marketplace change, challenges, interruptions, operating in a world of evolving opportunities (in all industries) makes business development a critical function for businesses with an end goal to be relevant, resilient and successful in a long-term timeframe (e.g. customer sales/service success, market share, financial performance and satisfying environmental and social goals).

It is important to have the right ***validated*** *value creation strategic plans and tactics of execution to fit the needs of your business at each phase in your business's growth lifecycle.*

It is about turning insight, knowledge and understanding into action. Start with believing that change is good, as long as your business model is constantly updated to comply:

- *To fit market demand.*
- *To adhere to evolving target markets and customer preferences.*
- *To constantly introduce productivity improvements.*
- *To keep business models fresh and viable.*

Change produces endless opportunities. Durable business development plans are the result of always operating in a growth mode to address these opportunities. That is the formula to reach and maintain lifecycle durability with justifiable business valuation.

Experience proves that positioning a business for success is best accomplished by following a synergistic program focused on continual business model modifications and the introduction of new paths for growth. Some of my favorite examples are as follows:

> Apple® Inc. became a multinational business success by offering an evolving business model with disruptive products and services.
>
> Starbucks® built market share through more than just selling coffee.

In this book *The Quest for Durabili*ty you will be introduced to a business development methodology (*The Business Puzzle Method*™ approach with *Just-In-Time Transition Planning (JITTP)* steps) to accomplish your business purpose, vision, mission and goals and communicate an optimistic view of the future. In addition, *The Business Puzzle Method*™ approach will help your business understand what is required to be a market leader structured for substantiated long-term profitable growth in all phases of your business and business model lifecycle!

* * *

Defining Business Development Application

Aligning business development and the operational business practices of functional organizations will stimulate durable lifecycle growth momentum needed to achieve targeted goals.

Perpetual *Business Development* is required in all phases of a business's lifecycle (startup, expansion and maturity). The secret to year-over-year durability success is to evolve business models with transitional action plans to fit changing industries and customer preferences.

In the simplest terms, my definition of *business development* is an ***entrepreneurial innovation creating process*** with activities that proactively enhance the growth of a business as needed to be a year-over-year durable business entity. It is NOT just about outperforming your competitors. It is about finding and traveling on a breakthrough path (s) to achieve a *durable lasting competitive advantage.*

The challenge of all business leaders is finding the best durable path (with short-term and longer-term compatibility) to fit their customer's requirements in their chosen industry.

Durable (lasting) success boils down to being continually ready to address change and challenges in a world of endless opportunities! It is about producing **durable business model monetization while achieving purpose and business goals consistent with environmental and social demands.**

Lifecycle Durability is about being prepared to boost business longevity by enhancing creativity, producing actionable strategies and tactics of execution needed to overcome challenges while addressing customer / marketplace opportunities.

Durable business success is about connecting to making timely, justifiable decisions within a supportive ecosystem. To accomplish this, a business needs a synergistic actionable framework for merging today's operational insight, understanding and knowledge (from all functional parts of the organization) with future transition foresight as a priority.

The Business Puzzle Method™ approach is based on business alignment of purpose, vision, mission and goals...made up of people from multi-functional teams...encompassing engaged multiple business disciplines working together to produce proactive contributions with collective impacts. Actively leveraging these capabilities is the heart of the customizable approach to business development (as included in *The Business Puzzle Method*™ approach) for development of justifiable competitive advantages.

Business development should not be a fragmented process

The Business Puzzle Method™ approach will help your business build expertise in subsectors of your business, in a collaborative team-oriented way to cultivate a year-over-year relevant, resilient, durable business. It is about dealing with change, challenges and creating new opportunities.

Business Development should be viewed as a ***Customer-First Opportunity Sourcing Resource (CFOSR)****, a Business Scaling Enabler driven by people sharing productive interactions in a belief system favoring a* ***Durability-Focused Mindset (DFM).***

The changing dynamics in all industries make it even more critical for your business to be well-positioned to respond to changes, challenges, and opportunities. No one knows for sure what the future holds for us. For this reason, the rules of engagement (internal and external to your business) will need to be creative, justifiable, flexible, and timely to migrate industry-specific insight and knowledge into realistic transition driven directions.

This book, *The Quest for Durability*, focuses on important value-added priorities (internal to your business as well as to the customer / marketplace) needed as integrated common ground for seamless short-term and longer-term success. To accomplish this, it is necessary to adopt a business development focused model to combine day-to-day activities with longer-term planning considerations. *The Business Puzzle Method*™ approach incorporates this capability. It is based on three primary pillars (the keys to true resiliency) to build and maintain a *Durable Lifecycle Competitive Advantage.*

All-Important Integral Components of *The Business Puzzle Method*™ Approach

- Perpetual Planning with Just-In-Time Transition Planning (JITTP) steps.
- Continuous Improvement of core capability strengths and weakness improvement initiatives.
- Tactical execution of validated strategic actions.
- Integration of strategic, financial and operational decisions and practices.

Perpetual Planning and Continuous Improvement together drive business value creation, lifecycle longevity and ultimately durability.

* * *

The Philosophy Behind "The Quest for Durability"

If you want your business to be a durable business in all lifecycle stages, your business (leaders, workforce, and partners) needs to uniformly think and act with a focus on reinforcing continuous durability practices and goals.

Fast growing businesses think differently about status quo business models. They are willing to continually move away from longstanding practices. They become new business pioneers in the applications needed to accelerate *business model creativity momentum*.

A durable business (one with predictable lifecycle longevity) requires an ability to see, plan and take actions (from multiple directions) beyond current circumstance, capabilities (business models) and realities...to achieve a profitable future. The "Quest for Durability" defines a way to manage a business in a world where change is and always will be inevitable.

A business's / organization's lasting durability depends on the ability to stay on the cutting edge of what customers prefer, what society needs in addition to what stakeholders and funding sources demand. There are specific pieces (I call puzzle pieces) that need to be addressed.

Durability involves filling goals while being focused on workforce beliefs and customer engagements that deliver a lasting competitive advantage needed for transformations consistent with the aims of the business.

* * *

Key Philosophical Characteristics for Lifecycle Durability Transformation

There are many determinants of a business's short-term and longer-term success. The key is to ensure your business does not get enamored by initial business model success as happens with some start-ups or gravitate to marketplace complacency and over confidence when in a more mature lifecycle stage. A balance between day-to-day operations and longer-term planning of the most crucial elements leading to lifecycle durability is necessary. There is no set formula to determine this mix. It is an output of a business's operational and business development decision-making processes reflecting the specifics of an individual industry. What is important is solving problems for customers via *Perpetual Planning* practices, not finding a place for new technologies.

Durability requires perpetual end-to-end lifecycle transitions and solutions.

THE CRUCIAL UNDERLYING ELEMENTS LEADING TO LIFECYCLE DURABILITY

Practice Perpetual Planning and Continuous Improvement of core capabilities to allow your business to grow on your terms within your preferred timeframes.

Prepare a prioritized pipeline of transitional customer-centric strategies and tactics of execution to always be relevant and resilient.

Provide an environment where a workforce can freely operate to produce business models with relevant products and services.

Encourage ongoing innovation and improvement through leadership and workforce training, empowerment and communication practices.

Build business relationships (internal & external to your business) to encourage cooperation, loyalty and trust.

Build lifecycle continuity by aligning short-term and longer-term strategic plans and tactical programs of execution.

Keep insight, understanding and foresight current by continually performing real-time landscape prospecting.

Create a business plan (with linked supporting plans) demonstrating compelling, justifiable, defensible strategic and tactical execution rationale.

Together, these underlying elements comprise a methodology for reinventing business models to make them durable (and other synergistic business development solutions needed) to deploy differentiated competitive advantages!

* * *

Lifecycle Durability Transformation (LDT) often requires significant changes in beliefs, norms, policies, practices and associations. Finding a way for your business to cope with and break down barriers is the collective purpose of this book. By adopting the philosophies contained in this book *The Quest for Durability / The Business Puzzle Method*™ approach will help your business install an appropriate methodology based on collaborative leadership practices needed to define, reach and maintain *lifecycle durability and reach its realistic potential.*

A business's entire workforce and associated colleagues need to constantly be in some portion of business transformation to build a culture of continual transformation transition.

The book - what does it do?

This book *The Quest for Durability* is a *must-have solution* about how to make your business an ongoing year-over-year relevant, resilient durable success. *The Quest for Durability* is for people who have big dreams and want to make them happen.

For this book to be helpful, think of what you want your business to be in 3, 5, 10 years from now. Think about what your business purpose will be, which business models you will be using, and what goals you will be pursuing. Now ask the question – how will I get there? What challenges will I be facing? What opportunities will be available? These are just some of the questions a business striving to be durable must answer.

In this highly competitive world, actionable planning for year-over-year *durability* is an imperative since business success in the marketplace is not a coincidence.

Ever wonder why some businesses perform better than others year-over-year?

Certain businesses have an innate ability to build and maintain connections (with customers, employees, partners, funding sources) to grow long-term *durable* businesses. Through my real-life experiences and education (formal and informal) I recognized patterns that make some businesses more successful than others. Success (e.g. year-over-year business durability) has to do with the ability to lead and connect with others. Businesses such as Apple® and Amazon® have learned this well.

In this book, I consolidated the behavioral patterns (soft influences) that drive *durability* success. Basically, it includes linked financial (hard influences) and nonfinancial (marketplace requirements, people resources, technology), strategic and tactical considerations when synergistically addressed produce effective outcomes...growth, profitability, extended lifecycles, market share, competitive advantages and of course a *durable* future. To make this happen, business development must deal with all aspects of business strategy, tactical execution, leadership, governance, business infrastructure / operational practices, product / service development, marketing and delivery, in addition to closing productivity performance gaps.

The problems any business has to face was summed up by one of the New York Yankees legends Yogi Berra. One of my favorite Yogi-isms nails it:

"The future ain't what it used to be."

My version...The future is a *Business Development* challenge that every business has to be prepared to address, sooner or later.

My years of experience and observation have clearly demonstrated that business durability (creating and maintaining value, growth, profits and customer solutions) is the number one challenge of businesses of all kinds, in all industries in all stages of development. *Durability* is the dividend received from translating actionable insight and innovation into long-term transitional strategies and tactics for implementation... creating ***Business Lifecycle Longevity (BLL) to produce Predictable Business Development outcomes.***

* * *

The key to making Business Lifecycle Longevity (BLL) happen is—- building and maintaining year-over-year relevancy, resiliency and durability.

Many businesses focus too much of their attention on short-term imperatives such as customer service and quarterly earnings. This approach will work for the purpose of holding a competitive advantage for a period of time until change, challenges and more relevant opportunities are adopted by competitors. Durability requires looking beyond past traditions and today's long-held thinking and *practices* to ascertain *Critical-Fit* for the future. Business operations and strategic planning should have a combined end in mind –year-over-year durability

Four fundamental pillars

The formula for being a growing durable business requires 1) constant evaluation, 2) synergistic structuring, 3) validation of marketplace solutions and 4) enabling operational capabilities to be relevant, resilient, flexible and timely…to meet the customer and marketplace circumstances of today and in the future – when performed consistently produces a true *competitive advantage.*

The Four Fundamental Pillars come together in a culture that is imaginative, innovative and flexible. Businesses that have organizational barriers and implementation roadblocks will not be able to execute even the best strategies in a timely manner.

I believe the legendary management consultant and writer Peter Drucker said it best.

"Culture eats strategy for breakfast."

* * *

A Culture of Continuous Improvement

Continuous Improvement to a business development practitioner means operating in a culture demanding continual innovative reinvention.

Getting your business's culture performing on a collaborative basis is one of the most important challenges a potential durable business will face. Collaborative performance cannot be only on a fix the problem / short-term basis, it has to be a *Continuous Improvement* activity (to avoid complacency) requiring resource and operational changes as strategies and tactical requirements demand. This is what I call having a *Continuous Cultural Refresh (CCR)* capability, a capability inherent in an innovative culture…so important for a business to be *durable*. Consider the following:

Year-over-year durability is the by-product of a knowledgeable, flexible, collaborative culture.

Necessary soft asset requirements for a durable actionable lifecycle business development culture:

- Forward-thinking people with a *Durability Focused Mindset (DFM).*
- A business operating in a culture receptive to change & capable of encouraging and implementing innovative transitions.
- Teams aware of marketplace & landscape realities around them.
- A desire to grow, maintain and protect a profitable, year-over-year durable business.
- Leadership / team / partnership competency.

Your workforce (direct and indirect) is your business's greatest asset… They make your business success happen! *Stated another way: a focused workforce operating in a collaborative culture will produce happy customers, a happy workforce, and happy shareholders producing desired results.*

Jeff Bezos, Executive Chairman of Amazon, periodically reemphasizes what he considers is a main reason for Amazon's potential success (first stated in his 1997 letter to shareholders).

- Maintaining a long-term focus.
- Obsessing over customer.
- Boldly innovating to meet those needs.

Sounds like a great philosophy!

Lifecycle Durability Building Principles Thoughts and Perspectives

Adherence to The Business Puzzle Method™ approach will produce a capability to succeed by addressing obstacles and challenges, while simultaneously pursuing opportunities.

Every day is the time to evaluate, design and implement strategic and tactical transitions leading to a durable, profitable business future by avoiding rambling business practices. It takes synergistic business development principles to produce a full range of activities essential for a business to be a year-over-year lifecycle durable business entity.

Following *The Business Puzzle Method*™ approach will make this possible.

Here are some of the customizable principles and practices contained in *The Business Puzzle Method*™ approach.

* * *

Perpetual Planning and Continuous Improvement

A business's ability to achieve durability is through *Perpetual Planning* and *Continuous Improvement* of core capabilities in conjunction with servicing day–to-day tasks and fulfilling short-term strategic business requirements. This is a synergistic approach to continually enhance positive outcome performance and operational effectiveness.

Durability Focused Mindset (DFM)

For a business to be durable, it needs thought-leadership and unity around purpose, vision, mission and goals. I call this having a *Durability Focused Mindset (DFM).* Keeping all (customers, leaders, employees, support organizations, partners, and funding sources) believing, engaged and participating in maintaining ongoing durability.

Seamless Transition Continuity

Business *durability* requires a merging of short-term and longer-term strategies and tactics of execution. It needs to be phased in to follow a path stimulating profitable growth and ensuring total business, business model and product / service lifecycle longevity.

Collaborative Decision-Making

One of the most important aspects of *The Business Puzzle Method*™ approach is the strength it adds to the *decision-making process*. *The Business Puzzle Method*™ approach favors agile, collaborative cross-functional team interactions to increase insight, understanding and foresight.

Perpetual Prospecting

In this rapidly changing world, keeping in touch with target market evolution (understanding customer preferences and expectations, defining customer contact methods, designing compelling brand messages) requires a business to constantly be aware of developments in real-time. Customer, marketplace and industry attractiveness will always be a moving target requiring continual reimaging of strategic direction to expand customer lists.

Always-Ready to Redirect

Advanced preparation for successful changes in strategic direction (pivoting) requires timely, flexible, validated responses as a strategic necessity. This requires constant rethinking, evaluation and option prioritization to always feature value-creating (total business and customer value propositions) business transformation strategies.

Communications and Connections

Businesses grow when you open multiple two-way lines of communication connections (team interactions, business networks, advertising / promotion campaigns, and marketplace touch points)...to advance insight, understanding and foresight your business has acquired or needs to acquire. People (internal and external to a business) need to buy in to your business's purpose, vision, mission and goals for your business to be a year-over-year durable business entity.

Development of Timely Budgeting and Financing Requirements

It is critically important to link strategic and tactical plans of execution relationships with financial requirements to ensure plans create accretive (contributing to growth) financial results. Linked assessments (strategic and financial) need to obtain lines of credit and financing must consider changes in working capital (receivables, inventory, payables) investment requirements, selling, general and administrative expenses, as they affect financial policies around revenue, earnings and cash flow.

Risk Mitigation

Add legitimacy and increase the acceptance of risk by having master migration plans (business models, growth programs, and product / service options) reinforced with backup contingency plans to be able to increase confidence, credibility and predictability in the future world of uncertainty. This approach will support how your business handles fiduciary responsibilities, creates superior economic valuations...all linked with clarifying strategic and tactical execution rationale and forecasted assumptions.

Strategy and Tactical Substantiation

Following *The Business Puzzle Method*™ approach will produce rationality, evidence and substantiation reasoning for strategic and tactical programs of execution. This is needed for implementing growth programs, obtaining line of credit financing, investor fundraising, and shareholder approval. Businesses that have not substantiated their strategies and tactics are condemned to yield to whatever is the position of others. Going forward, consideration must also be given to Environmental, Social and Governance (ESG) ramifications.

To Conclude...

Durable businesses need to focus on more than just making money. Following *The Business Puzzle Method*™ approach will facilitate creating and maintaining a value-creating synchronized (mutually reinforcing) blueprint for your business to be a successful *durable* business entity... thus complementing your business's purpose, vision, mission and goals.

I wrote this book to give *business development entrepreneurs* a methodology to overcome perceived current and future limitations...as needed to start, develop and grow their business. Business Development success requires identification, assembly and implementation of multiple combinations of piece parts (like in a jigsaw puzzle) to create and maintain a year-over-year durable business.

Read on!

Preface

Who Should Read This Book & Why

Making a business lifecycle durable is a prerequisite to developing and maintaining a perpetual competitive advantage.

Whether your business is a lifestyle small business or a Fortune 500 business, you need a program to be relevant, resilient and durable over time. Yes, it takes a commitment of time, money, people and other resources, but without a focus beyond the near-term, your business will perpetually be subject to change, challenges and interruptions and possible bankruptcy. My experiences and industry observations prove this to be true.

"If you fail to plan, you are planning to fail."—Benjamin Franklin

I am writing this book for new business entrepreneurs and for established businesspeople who are looking to transform their businesses to evolve from a culture focused solely on short-term goals (quarterly earnings) to emerging long-term continuity in line with needs (market based) for a durable future...my message is simple - things have to change to produce a durable business!

In this book, I will discuss a business development methodology (*The Business Puzzle Method*™ approach) to facilitate an evolution to a profitable, purposeful and successful future.

This Book Presents a Business Development Program for All Businesses and Organizations (regardless of size and lifecycle maturity) seeking Year-Over-Year Marketplace Durability – e.g.

Durability is about leadership, teams and partnerships working together.

Various types of people who could benefit from this book:

- Business owners and C-suite executives
- Entrepreneurial / intrapreneurial workforce leaders
- Sales and marketing functions
- Service businesses
- Consultants and advisors
- Investors and funding sources
- Academic professionals
- Product managers
- Incubator managers
- Government employees

Yes, anybody in some aspect of business development will benefit from reading and implementing the practices in this book.

I began this book by asking the thought-provoking question...what makes successful businesses successful? I found examples to this question throughout my own career experiences. A simplified answer is that lifecycle **durable** business success is based on having the right strategies in place at the right time, implementing actionable tactics and having a synergistic short-term and long-term perspective.

Entrepreneurs and every person in some aspect of ***Business Development*** needs to read this book. It will help increase your business's ability to be **relevant, resilient** and **durable.** It is a book with an application for all phases of a business's lifecycle. In addition, this book is a great resource to help your business keep pace with and stay ahead of marketplace evolution!

The Quest for Durability is a book applicable for entrepreneurs and intrapreneurs (an entrepreneur inside of a business or organization) in businesses and organizations in all stages of lifecycle growth:

- Startups
- Early stages
- Expansion stages
- Mature stages

PLANNING TO NAVIGATE REALITY

The Quest for Durability will help your business visualize, design and formulate a path to long-term success. I summarized what I believe should be the *Business Development* goal of every successful business – **A game plan to be consistently Relevant, Resilient and Durable.**

Realities to consider:

- *Technology will change the way we live and work.*
- *The world will be even more connected.*
- *Globalization will open new opportunities for growth.*
- *Rapid innovation will be pursued in all industries.*
- *Environmental and social ramifications will be a marketing priority.*
- *Generational differences will evolve to produce new preferences.*

These glittering generalities may or may not be applicable for your particular business. However, when considering the evolutional developments in your industry...that fit your business purpose, vision, mission and goals...you must first accept the fact that the world is changing rapidly and that your legacy business models, products and services have a limited *lifecycle longevity*. This is also true for your business in total. If you don't believe me, try to shop at a Sears store today. They were following traditional status quo strategies, slow to react to change and were risk aware. Many businesses have the same dilemma...they are not keeping pace with what is needed to be *continually relevant*.

Ask the questions – at what point in their *lifecycle* are your business offerings operating? Is this consistent with plans? Does your business have validated follow-on plans? Are your business models justifiably viable beyond a short-term timeframe? What is your business's strategic comfort zone?

Why not design a durable competitive advantage for your business?

Marketplace change is inevitable, and opportunities are endless...accept those facts of reality and add increased insight, flexibility and timing response to your *Business Development* process by following *The Business Puzzle Method*™ approach as included in this book *The Quest for Durability*. It is about winning and retaining a *Competitive Advantage* in the marketplace:

"It's not the will to win, but the will to prepare to win that makes a difference."—Bear Bryant, University of Alabama football coach

Sounds like great advice for your business as well!

Legacy business models (startups and expansion businesses alike) all have a need for *Perpetual Planning* practices, plus core business *Continuous Improvement* initiatives and an end product of *evidence-based substantiation* strategies and tactics leading to year-over-year *relevancy, resiliency* and *durability*.

Perpetual planning...means that your business must be laser focused to solve its own unique future requirements before the future arrives.

Continuous Improvement of core capabilities...means that your business must practice continual innovation to address change, improve and update processes and practices of core business capabilities.

Evidence-Based Substantiation...means having justifiable strategic and tactical execution rationale needed to convince others of your business's viability.

In summary: Being well prepared is the bedrock for being durable. Success in today's world and in the future world will require perpetual planning (combined with timely plan execution) and modifications of how your business will operate (business models, business plans, technological approaches and people requirements) in order for your business to be year-over-year relevant, resilient and durable.

Actionable planning is where durability originates.

Designing Your Business for Durability

(Planning and executing for purpose, stability, growth, value creation and profitability)

Your business's future should include a constant decision-making capability to determine what to do now, what to do later or not at all.

Your business's future should not be set in stone - it needs to be a fluid, constant learning, development and implementation activity focused on improving results and implementing business development durability oriented strategic and tactical execution options.

Every *durable* business has to learn to outpace change and competitive pressures while addressing opportunities...following clear purpose and direction.

The durability option window is in a path always open.

It is a reality - opportunities in all industries will always be endless. Students in school today will be working in jobs not even envisioned today. The extent of new durable opportunities will constantly be evolving!

Understanding and following this futuristic type of thinking is what makes great visionaries successful. Elon Musk reinvented the automobile business by pursing a vision for electric vehicles. He developed new methods of space exploration beyond those practiced by NASA.

Successful leaders and a workforce from all parts of a business can influence the future of their business by also having an open innovative vision of what their organizational purpose can be. Possibilities are infinite. History has shown this to us time and time again.

Harnessing innovative visions is the task of great leadership. Building a plan to deliver durable exceptional performance is the perpetual business development task needed.

This requires continually providing insights useful to advance relevancy and resiliency needed to sustain profitable growth. Highly successful businesses have learned to follow such an approach as needed to develop and to reinforce strategy, design and implementation.
A meandering strategic direction or a business built on ONE strength does not make for a long-term successful business. Interrelated and interdependent unified parts (working together) make business performance a predictable success. Furthermore, a one product company will seldom be durable. It is always subject to the next superior technology that eclipses it. Investors call these a business with a "One-Trick Pony." Business model diversification is generally preferred for a business to be considered having long-term durability.

WHY CALL IT A PUZZLE?

I adopted the analogy of a puzzle since my *business development* method *(The Business Puzzle Method™ approach)* is in some ways similar to completing a jigsaw puzzle where each puzzle piece adds to the completion of a work product. Putting the right pieces together makes strategies and tactical programs of execution succeed.

Being stuck in the past will make your business vulnerable, leading to loss of market share, dilution of competitive advantages, being considered a candidate for takeover at decreased valuations, or even bankruptcy. Just look at businesses such as RadioShack, Circuit City and Sears. They don't exist today even though they all had successful business models and significant market share in the past.

Your business needs a doable, flexible, timely and informed finely tuned sense of purpose, vision, mission and goals, reflective of the needs of the world of today and into the future...that culminates in achievement of successful interwoven transformational strategies and tactics of execution.

This requires a frequent "checkup." The world is constantly telling you something. Having the ability to capture these messages, evaluate and assemble them in a usable, clearly understood format (collaboratively working together) is an innovative formula (reaching beyond preconceived notions) for preparing paths for a year-over-year *durable* future.

Read on to embrace the major theme of this book, *The Quest for Durability,* featuring *The Business Puzzle Method*™ *approach*, to develop, enable and maintain viable strategies and tactics supporting durable competitive advantages while generating accretive (incremental growth) revenue, operational performance productivity and financial performance.

By following The Business Puzzle Method™ *approach to your business planning and operational practices...as a rational way to create year-over-year value creation, growth and lasting durability...will get your business where it needs to be in order to succeed. The path to success is in the details.*

Try It!

Prologue

My fascination with the power of perpetual planning and continuous improvement started at a very early age. It was knowledge I absorbed early in my life. They are now part of what I call my Business Development Syllabus (BDS).

When I was a Cub Scout, our pack went on a field trip to the local Buick, Oldsmobile, and Pontiac (BOP) General Motors (GM) assembly plant in NJ. (Yes, the Oldsmobile and the Pontiac are no longer offered by GM). They assembled three makes and multiple models and colors of automobiles simultaneously in one facility. I watched in amazement as assembly parts came from different locations in the building via overhead cranes to exactly the predetermined assembly location where workers assembled the automobiles a section at a time. I was mesmerized. How could so much happen so efficiently?

I witnessed how the BOP engineers solved production problems by providing a combination of people initiatives and technology-based solutions to the task of automobile assembly. I concluded that a dysfunctional team could not meet timelines needed to deliver the latest models to the marketplace when needed. Nor could this occur without a significant amount of advanced planning, cross-functional cooperation and perseverance to complete a high priority tactical goal.

I remember sitting around my kitchen table where I subsequently discussed this field trip with my father. We had an opportunity to pause and reflect.

He emphasized that these lessons could also apply to my personal life. He suggested I test this concept by joining the Boy Scouts. I did so (setting a challenging goal) and with the help of my fellow scouts and scout leaders during extended stays at a Boy Scout camp became a 14-year-old Eagle Scout. Today, I consider this one of my earliest major accomplishments. I did this by operating in a culture of cooperation and shared knowledge. My first experience in an agile environment...it works.

These early experiences of my youth drew me to the obsession of always being aware of the need for Perpetual Planning and actionable Continuous Improvement to advance innovation, pursue a range of opportunities, solve challenges of all kinds and reach specific goals. For me, these practices, principles and disciplines that I experienced provided a guiding light applicable for businesses and organizations in all lifecycle phases of growth...when followed will define a path for relevancy, resiliency and year-over-year durability. They are part of my personal Business Development Syllabus.

I applied this baseline thinking throughout my career as needed to respond to the expected and the unexpected...read on and share my learnings from my journey - in pursuit of "The Quest for Durability."

* * *

Introduction

(An Early Lesson In Business Development)

I would like to begin with a personal story. Early in my career, while working in a major corporation, I was confronted with a situation that taught me that I did not know the implementation steps needed to bring a new business, a new business model and a new product /service to the marketplace. I was well educated in the academic disciplines normally taught by universities at that time, but I did not understand how to put my learnings together to build a business in a culture not receptive to employee innovative feedback. Being a new employee, this was a challenge I had not anticipated.

I had a business idea for my company and started where most people start by preparing a draft *Business Plan.* I subsequently presented my idea and draft business plan to the people in my company responsible for strategy development. They were quick to tell me that my idea was outside of the scope of the approved corporate business strategy and that they could not see how it could ever be a fit. I was discouraged and set my idea aside to resume the activities of completing my current job responsibilities. Later it occurred to me that by listening to the advice from the strategy development organization, I had missed an ENORMOUS opportunity. My product idea was for remote meter reading, which is now utilized by most utilities around the world. If only I had known how to develop, design, manufacture, sell/service, and fund this relatively simple technological concept, I would definitely be in a different place today. This was a learning experience for sure. I was an entrepreneur in an organization that was not receptive to entrepreneurial thinking. Yes, this was an obvious learning experience I will never forget...

If you believe you don't know how to do something, it will never appear as one of your accomplishments.

I now understand the cultural influences and other reasons for their reluctance to support my idea. In summary, the culture of the company where I worked was an impediment to creative innovative thinking. The case in point:

- Strategic plans were developed by top management leaving implementation to line management (e.g. relatively no functional organization feedback and collaboration).

- Products and services were only developed by an organization internal to the company (e.g. not invented here philosophy).

- Due to a monopoly market position, new *Business Model* and product/service introductions were not a priority (e.g. regulatory protection discouraged competition).

- Adherence to rigid departmental job descriptions and responsibilities (e.g. no emphasis on teamwork and collaboration).

Yes, life's experiences are eye openers! Knowing what I know today, I would have filed patents and set out to develop a *Business Plan* to launch a new commercialization solution. These kinds of experiences were the stimulant and origin of *The Business Puzzle Method*™ approach. They illuminated what was missing from so many legacy businesses and why they tended to stagnate rather than to grow.

In The Beginning

The idea for this book started years ago, early in my professional career, when I was in attendance at a motivational seminar. The presenter suggested the idea of keeping an "Idea Book," to write down ideas as encountered. Of course, today these ideas can be captured on laptops, thumb drives or other more contemporary methods if desired. I realized that a process such as this (Idea Book like documentation) is a great way to capture innovative ideas and integrate them within an *Agile* strategic planning processes. I designed *The Business Puzzle Method*™ approach to reflect my experience and wisdom to aid entrepreneurs, business leaders and anyone looking to grow their business or organization to reach year-over-year durable, profitable growth beyond current day performance outcomes, or to guide the planning process needed for early stage and startup businesses.

In my journey in the business world, I experienced many recurring reasons as to why all businesses have *Business Models* that are vulnerable! On-going changes are inevitable requiring the ability to think beyond today in order to survive in the business world. All *Business Models* have lifecycles that frequently need to be updated. Also, companies often ignore technical advancements and customer preference changes due to operating within an inflexible cultural mindset and by following business process methodologies outdated by technology advances.

At this point I would like to reemphasize - durability requires pursuing innovation and actionable business model implementation to be CONSTANTLY relevant and resilient. History is full of examples of failed businesses and/or businesses with significant downturns that did not. Planning should include consideration for responsiveness to possible downturns.

One of the most documented examples is included in the story of the demise of Blockbuster, a video rental chain. Their strategic planning and tactical execution in their marketplace did not consider transition options needed in their changing, evolving marketplace. They even had an opportunity to acquire Netflix®, which would have put them in the then new, rapidly growing video-streaming business.

Other business trapped in their status quo business strategies:

- Xerox® chose to remain in their core copier business rather than actively commercialize their R&D capabilities developed at their Palo Alto Research Center (PARC).

- Kodak® chose to focus on the photo film business instead of pursuing digital technologies.

Ignoring updating of what I call LIFECYCLE LONGEVITY REQUIREMENTS (LLR) is a fatal flaw of many failed businesses. It affects businesses of all sizes. Even well-established S&P 500 companies are not immune from this requirement. The listed S&P companies are experiencing churn and shorter life-spans due in part to disruptive innovation impacting market value in a changing world. No company of any size is immune to the need to be continually (year-over-year) relevant. Creative purposeful innovation is the solution for long-term durability. Just look at which companies have the highest values today, compared to 20 years ago. They are mostly the disruptive upstarts like Amazon, Apple, Google, etc.

Polaroid (a company selling an instant photo capability) lost out to the success of digital camera capabilities.

Toys R Us (a toy retail operation) lost out due in part to an e-commerce world of changing customer buying preference. In addition to not keeping pace with their business model (brick and mortar vs. e-commerce), the company did not keep pace with evolving consumer preferences that favored electronic gaming over traditional toys.

All businesses have business model / product and service lifecycles. The key to total business durability is managing these lifecycles to be relevant and resilient in rapidly changing marketplaces.

Root-Causes and Challenges

Companies that fail in the marketplace generally claim that the reason they fail is that they ran out of money. Actually, there are many "root-causes" blocking their ability to generate sufficient organic funding (internally generated cash flow) or to attract external financing or be awarded grant support. For a business to survive the challenges and obstacles while addressing opportunities for growth, they fundamentally need to have an innovative vision for the future, be flexible and adaptable, and meet customer (B2C) and buyer (B2B) expectations in a timely manner. Marketplace windows of opportunities are not open forever! To do this, a company needs marketing execution programs addressing the right goals for the right reasons at the right time... leading to customer and buyer satisfaction. Yes, it is easier said than done but certainly doable. Consider that...

- Amazon started as an on-line bookseller. Today it is a multinational business operating on e-commerce, digital streaming, cloud computing and artificial intelligence.

- Apple started selling a simple personal computer. Today it is a multinational business operating in consumer electronics, personal computers, servers, tablets and smartphones.

- Facebook (Meta) was once focused solely on a service for college students and is now poised to bring us into the metaverse for immersive experiential marketing.

In a business's lifecycle, it is a reality of the business world to anticipate stressful periods of time when running out of money (cash flow issues) or not having adequate money to operate a business will be a challenge. It could be for such things as business cycles, growth program implementation, regulations, or just the influences of the economy. For this reason, ongoing business planning (with actionable tactical programs of execution) needs to be a continuous process for a business to be durable thus creating a logical, timely and lasting competitive advantages...a practice mastered by highly successful fast-growing businesses. You can be sure they have explicit plans!

Well thought out plans are your business's way to communicate your business's value to the marketplace and to interested audiences of all types (workforce, partners, funding sources).

Lifecycle Durability success is very dependent on having the right plans in place, in the right market segments at the right time.

TIMING is a critical factor driving business success.

You may recall an online business that sold pet accessories and supplies called Pets.com. At the time, this was a unique business model positioning strategy. Pets.com even had an IPO. Unfortunately, they went out of business in 2000. My theory (ignoring other reasons Pets.com failed) is that they were trying to sell by following an internet direct to customer business model in an age where e-commerce sales was not a popular mode of sales for pet foods. Their business model did not fit the marketplace of that time and therefore Pets.com was not able to obtain the revenue needed to cover infrastructure cost requirements.

Today the marketplace is constantly changing. Customer purchase preferences have accepted e-commerce as a way to purchase pet products, along with other product lines. Chewy.com, an e-commerce retailer (owned by PetSmart) selling pet goods has the advantage of being in existence when e-commerce is an accepted way for consumers to shop. Yes, business success is often all about timing!

The Business Puzzle Method™ approach – Always be in a Continuous Commercialization Mode (CCM).

Fast growing businesses are constantly in what I call a **Continuous Commercialization Mode (CCM)** defined as producing innovative transformation growth strategies and tactics plus a RESET of existing business models as needed. Consider how quickly manufacturers update your mobile phone with new models and new features. They want you to be in a constant buying mode.

In my experience, a company striving for leadership as a company with a true competitive advantage needs to operate in an innovative *perpetual planning mode*, always-ready to introduce product and service customer solutions, or new or improved value-creating *Business Model* options that are adaptable to current marketplace challenges and opportunities. These can be either disruptive or as enhancements needed to increase customer advantage, increase market share and corporate value.

Apple comes to mind as a business constantly practicing ongoing innovative business development continually releasing disruptive marketplace solutions. They include a portfolio of consumer electronics, software and services delivered into the marketplace per a well-conceived strategic planning and tactical execution program—an excellent role model!

Amazon Web Services (AWS) continually releases a product / service portfolio of creative reimagined cloud-based customer solutions.

Adding strategies and tactics beyond traditional core business capabilities is an approach for growth and resiliency that is pursued by many of the fastest growing businesses. It does not have to be a complex capability.

Take the example of Uber Technologies®, a transportation company that built a disruptive way to improve ride-hailing taxi services.

Problem: Taxi service and public transportation are not always available or a preferred mode of transportation.

Uber Market Prospecting Conclusions:

- Customer need verified.
- Taxis service is often a preferred mode of transportation.
- Global Positioning System (GPS) capability existed to expedite finding customer and destination locations.
- Cell phone service offered convenience for contact purposes.

Uber Transition Strategy & Tactics:

- Focused a mission on rider convenience.
- Built an app-based communication platform.

- Added cell phone connections as a prime means of communication.

- Added call centers to expedite customer transportation requests.

- Added payment plans with payment options.

Sometimes the *CCM* change can be as simple as changing packaging. Operating in a **Continuous Commercialization Mode (CCM)**...adding new products and / or services...can be as simple as a new way of thinking strategically. As an example, the Heinz® ketchup company introducing the inverted ketchup container. It solved the customer perceived problem of ketchup pouring very slowly. This marketing practice established a new industry standard for packaging.

The foundation of resiliency is the ability to keep business models viable with new or improved transition strategies, tactics and marketplace offerings. Uber was highly successful in accomplishing this. This is another example of a business operating in a ***Continuous Commercialization Mode (CCM).***

The Business Puzzle Method™ approach addresses a full spectrum of strategic and tactical topics from vision direction, culture requirements, team interactions, marketing and customer engagement tactics, through growth strategic options of interest to investors, funding sources, strategic partners, and other stakeholders.

Successful performance outcomes are based on innovation principles... to define and create actions to make things happen! As you will see later in this book, by following *The Business Puzzle Method*™ approach, principles and processes, it will be possible to reduce risk perceptions and be *Outcome Predicable*, by explaining paths to defend year-over-year durable growth and profitability.

Lack of clarity and absence of business plan substantiation will cause potential customers and evaluators assessing your business (customers, shareholders, investors) to discount the credibility of your business model and your business plans.

*　*　*

Mitigating Business Risk

Every business has a degree of uncertainty about the future. Change, challenges, interruptions and opportunities will continually appear going forward. *Risks* are derived from many different places (i.e. competition inroads, financial performance, regulatory compliance, technology advancements, business model acceptance, and natural catastrophes).

The durability secret to mitigate risk is to have a game plan (s) to deal with possible *Business Stagnation* and / or *Business Disruptions*. Every business will at certain points in its lifecycle have to deal with risk issues. It's a reality!

Risk mitigation considerations need to be part of a risk management program of perpetual strategic transition planning and execution for a business to be durable.

Following *The Business Puzzle Method*™ approach produces ongoing *risk management solutions*... a prudent proactive way to plan for and be ready to react when risk situations impact your business.

When I was in the Merger & Acquisition (M&A) business, I always looked for *Risk Mitigation Plans*. They told me to what extent the leadership team understood the landscape in which they operate or plan to operate. It is amazing how the quality of *Risk Management* solutions will also impact valuations during negotiation discussions for those seeking either growth capital or an acquisition.

Durability is believable when your business can justify that it is operating from a position of sustainable strength.

Experience proves that planning to avoid or react to risk occurrences is a mission-critical capability of leaders in strategic and tactical business development disciplines. They need to identify, evaluate and plan for alternative courses of action, build redirect (pivot) strategic direction and ensure that execution plans are timely and feasible. This capability needs to be a continuous disciplined process focused on the foundational principles of *The Business Puzzle Method* approach. Consider the following in summary:

Continuously prepare for change, disruptions and opportunities...perpetual planning and continuous improvement of core capabilities.
Plan to reduce risk as much as possible...ongoing marketplace prospecting, performance monitoring and evaluation, collaborative decision-making to be continually relevant, resilient and durable.

Have backup plans for use when needed... alternate business model migration blueprints, contingency plans, substantiation for change in direction (pivoting) and business growth rationale formulation.

Plan to regularly introduce phased-in business models and product/service Migration Plans to stay ahead of pending changes and the competitive actions.

Business development...that includes validated risk mitigation strategies and tactics...will give your business the in-depth knowledge and competencies needed to address threats and pursue creative opportunities.

* * *

DEFINING LIFCYCLE DURABILITY

Durability is about understanding and reacting strategically...in a timely, feasible manner...in the marketplace to the abundance of business options available and potentially available on the horizon.

It takes more than persistence to make a business successful...it takes preparation and a synergistic playbook of actions to navigate changes, challenges and obstacles while addressing opportunities - concurrently with day-to-day business requirements. Let's get started by defining *durability* from a *business development* perspective.

A *durable* business / organization is one that has the ability to thrive and grow over time by possessing the resources, assets and insight to respond to change, challenges, and interruptions while being able to respond to opportunities in a timely manner. It represents a high degree of permanency, confidence and value...

IT'S NOT A ONE-SIZE-FITS-ALL SOLUTION

We have all heard the expression, "beauty is in the eyes of the beholder." This is true for businesses as well, especially as it pertains to understanding paths to durability. It is about how perceived benefits are measured and perceptions of the strategic value of transformation strategies and tactics of execution are interpreted.

Durability is about crafting lifecycle business endurance confidence.

One of the realities of the business world is that your business is constantly being vetted...by customers, current and future employees, investors, funding sources and even competitors. A business's durable true worth should always be presented to reflect multiple value perspectives.

Durability is made possible due to individual decision-making preferences and perspectives by those both inside and outside of your business.

SOME DIFFERENT PERSPECTIVES

- Marketing and salespeople will favor customer engagement practices.
- Bank evaluators will favor P&L, balance Sheet and cash flow projections.
- Financial investors will be looking for return on investment (ROI).
- Strategic investors will be interested in enhancing their own strategic models.

Long-term innovation-based business decisions are almost never based on one piece of information alone. They are based on multiple types of insight, knowledge and understanding.

This is best accomplished by taking basic planning steps to define, prioritize and focus on your business's *Preferred Strategic Purpose (PSP),* a work product possible by following *The Quest for Durability / The Business Puzzle Method*™ approach.

Durability needs to address the things that interested parties (customers, workforce, loan services, and partners) normally associate with in their assessments.

People evaluating a business consider success for today and the future, from their specific perspective of continuous growth drivers. I recommend practicing what I call *VALUATION MANAGEMENT PRACTICES (VMP).* Consider business influences beyond accounting applications and financial statement performance to maximize a business's appeal.

The TV show "Shark Tank" features individual investors who are being asked to invest in startup businesses. The one question the presenters are asked (but rarely answer) is why is your business valued at such a high value? We hear this question often during our activities in the investor community. Valuation surely is a key point of negotiation that we deal with when wearing our investor hat...in addition to being drivers of points of information important to substantiate strategy needed for a business to be considered durable.

I identified the three influences that are inextricably linked...they impact value and the perception of durability potential:

Customer / User Value: Continually prospecting - via touchpoints for target customer preference, extent of customer needs requirements, customer engagement options and sales practices scenarios.

Stakeholder Value: Culture alignment - Extent of management, employee, sponsor, partner and funding source confidence and risk tolerance courses of action.

Business Value: Substantiation - of Business model / product & service lifecycle longevity drivers, dollar valuation of the business and risk mitigation strategies.

An example is the unicorn phenomena. Unicorns are privately held startup businesses valued at over US $1 billion. Typically, these businesses **are not profitable** in their early stages of growth. People invest in unicorns primarily based on perceived Customer/User, Stakeholder and Business value. Financial profitability is assumed to be achieved as a future outcome. Unicorns are viewed as businesses with high growth potential and long-term market potential. Unicorn business viability is viewed as delivering a future high potential opportunity (relevancy, resilience and lifecycle durability). Companies such as Apple, Google, Facebook (Meta) were once unicorns.

Business durability decisions need to be based on more than financial numbers.

* * *

BEING DURABILITY FIT (DF)

Creating business value is about creating benefit conclusions from people with their own unique perspectives about what is important to them.

It is about the substantiation of business and landscape facts as the foundation for endurance, durability and justifying business valuation (marketplace benefits and business worth). Which facts are most important depends on your industry and your specific business stage of development... startup, expansion or a mature business. These considerations are part of what I call being *Durability Fit (DF)*. If not adequately addressed, they will become barriers to transformational success and your business's ability to raise fresh capital. Being *Durability Fit (DF)* is a growth strategy imperative for your business to justify transitional strategies and supporting tactics of all kinds.

Durability is about using insight, understanding and foresight to create value for customers, stakeholders, shareholders, partners and all others interested in participating in business growth industries.

This book *The Quest for Durability* represents a new *business development* perspective to reach and maintain business year-over-year long-term *durability*. It explains the key elements and a framework important to create and maintain a *Durable Competitive Advantage (DCA)*.

The Bridge to Durability

There are two important steps needed for a business to be considered *durable*. They are year-over-year ***relevancy*** and ***resiliency***. Let's define and examine these two critical factors. Together, relevancy and resiliency are the key capabilities to produce a predictable, year-over-year durable business.

Critical Factor #1: Relevancy Clarification

Relevancy (from a business development perspective) is the ability to relate to customer and marketplace needs and desires and the purpose of a business entity.

Think of relevancy as having a strong customer focused business model as reflected in a strong brand following, producing new and repeat sales. Relevancy is the key differentiator that makes a marketing model work.

Think of resiliency as the ability to consistently react to change, challenges, setbacks and new opportunities in a timely manner (when the window of opportunity is open). It represents having the relentless ability to protect current and planned business models and grow according to plans.

Step one: A business must be *relevant* and stay *relevant!*

We can measure this by the extent of customer following of a business's brand reputation. Key for a business to grow (or even survive) is the need to be perceived as *relevant*...for instance, solving a pertinent customer need, delivering a product / service in a manner preferred by-customers addressing unique needs in target markets.

In this fast-changing world, being a *relevant* business means constantly adjusting and / or influencing change with disruptive products / services. Being *relevant* is a state of being that can have a short-term lifecycle, or can have lasting value when managed (designed, tracked, measured and analyzed) and considered a significant influencer of *durability*.

For example, retail businesses that migrated to e-commerce vs staying with only brick and mortar retail locations modified their business models to meet the changing preferences of targeted customers. Amazon, at the time of this writing is clearly the industry leader. Other permutations of e-commerce strategy have evolved.

Walmart® has combined e-commerce with brick-and-mortar store operations. Placing an order online can be picked up at the store. This strategy works because Walmart customers live in a close proximity to the store making pickup at the brick-and-mortar location an easy solution. Combining this strategy with the addition of adding grocery sales simply increases the frequency need for a purchase, making Walmart shopping an even more relevant customer solution.

Step two: A business must be *resilient* to have year-over-year staying power!

This requires being able to respond to changes, challenges and opportunities quickly with validated and timely strategies and tactics. A well-informed stellar organization working collaboratively as a team is the necessary formula for building and maintaining a capacity for transformative change...a necessary requirement for a business to have *resiliency*. This is the heart of the benefit your business will experience by following *The Business Puzzle Method*™ approach as a durability enabler.

Critical Factor #2: Resiliency Clarification

Resiliency is the ability to understand, adapt and respond strategically and tactically to the changing and expanding world over time.

Let's define resiliency (from a business development perspective) as preparing for year-over-year continuity of business purpose, vision, mission and goals. Resiliency is the result of planned performance for goal achievement into the future. It requires having operational components continuously ready to achieve and / or exceed performance plans and expectations. Business development that conforms to this resiliency definition produces year-over-year S*trategic Continuity* and the ability for a productive change in strategic direction often called pivoting.

Resiliency requires the ability for readjustment of business direction regardless of the source of change or a disruption.

Resiliency is not just about producing year-over-year viable business models. *Resiliency* is also a necessary capability for what I call *Risk Management Preparedness (RMP)*...a necessary capability to ensure *Business Continuity*. *Business Resiliency* would include recovery capabilities from such things as natural disasters, changing government regulations, social unrest, severe economic downturns and pandemics causing business / service disruptions requiring preservation and restoration.

One of my evaluation criteria of *Business Pla*n strength is the extent of *Business Continuity Resiliency* that is built into the plan. *Risk Management Preparation (RMP)* is necessary to protect stakeholder interests, brand reputations and other factors that influence business value and completion of a business's mission. *Resiliency* can be preserved by designing strategic programs in many ways that would be appropriate for whatever industry your business intends to operate. For example...

The telecom business emphasizes redundancy of telecom capabilities Companies often develop alternate supply chain routes to ensure adequate pipelines. Potential investors want to see this contingency. Software companies offer data replication capabilities as a backup capability.

Going forward, developing *resiliency capabilities* leading to *business continuity* is more than disaster recovery. It should be dealt with as an essential component of strategic planning to secure *full lifecycle durability*.

Resiliency happens when following Perpetual Planning and pursuing Continuous Improvement initiatives as well as efficient operational business practices.

Strategic resiliency is best maintained by combining *Continuous Commercialization Mode* (CCM) practices...as previously discussed...to strengthening a business model and to be prepared to operate with a flexible *Perpetual Reset* capability to meet timely changes, challenges and opportunities. These are best business practices to follow, lessons included in *The Business Puzzle Method*™ approach.

Goal achievement is about having a vision and preparing and executing a way to make it happen in response to planned and unplanned changes, challenges and interruptions.

Consider, retail business that had e-commerce capabilities were the most likely to survive the COVID – 19 pandemic. Businesses such as Peloton® (home gym equipment) benefited (for a period of time) from the work at home mandates by modifying their delivery and supply chain to meet increased demands. I doubt anyone would claim they had forecasted the global impact of the COVID-19 pandemic. However, having flexibility in their planning process allowed many businesses to survive and even grow. Planning for alternate supply chain routes was a necessity for companies such as Clorox's (a cleaning products company) needs to meet the demand for cleaning supplies.

Perpetual Planning and *Continuous Improvement* (of core capabilities) principles and actions represent the "glue" needed keep a business *relevant* and *resilient* and therefore ultimately on the path to justifiable *durability.* It allows for having justifiable migration plans to safely move beyond business-as-usual business models either by design or because of competitive necessity.

Lastly, this book, *The Quest for Durability*, presents *The Business Puzzle Method*™ approach which features 11 fundamental principles...which I call ***puzzle pieces principles***... a metaphor covering synergistic necessities needed to create and position your business to be *relevant, resilient*, and *durable* over time. Many of these rules will be known to readers. The purpose of *The Business Puzzle Method*™ approach is to encourage adopting a business development synergistic framework while stimulating a dialog that will efficiently keep your business on a perennial path to a predictable, successful future. It is designed to be a best practice management / leadership methodology to bring together technical and nontechnical ideas, insights and knowledge for such things as needed for B2B (business-to-business) and B2C (business-to-consumer) applications leading to customer solutions.

Following *The Business Puzzle Method*™ approach will help your business be focused on your most important actionable aspects of business development... thus avoiding distractions and loss of your business's competitive advantage. Following *The Business Puzzle Method*™ approach will keep your business linked to those things that affect your business's future…with a special emphasis on reading the marketplace for factors affecting growth trajectories, financial gains, business model lifecycle duration, strategy and tactical formulation and value creation (total business and marketplace). Following *The Business Puzzle Method*™ approach will increase your business's ability to identify and develop justification important to mitigate perceived risk about your business transition strategies. It will produce a road map for year-over-year durability.

Businesses are successful due to preparation of actionable innovative growth transformation plans and substantiated rationale for plan execution.

Chapter 1. The Power of Belief-Alignment

(An Essential Element For Durability)

Business Development transformation is not just about delivering sales and service offerings; it is also about why the sales transaction occurred in a particular customer preference choice.

Keeping Mindsets Relevant

What are the influences that foster business durability? It starts with *Beliefs...for the purpose of this example that includes perceptions, opinions and conversations...they are* the "Secret Sauce" as drivers of behaviors:

- You favor one business over another, based on beliefs that reinforce confidence, trust, values and experiences.
- You make purchase decisions based on beliefs addressing such things as shopping preferences, quality and convenience.
- Your organization embraces a mindset of innovation because they *believe* in your vision, mission and purpose.
- You follow strategies based on beliefs that one strategy is better than another.

Since the world is constantly changing and evolving, so are both consumers and business customers' preferences, needs, wants and desires.

I call this ***Belief-ALIGNMENT***...which defines why people respond differently to various kinds of advertising, promotions and omnichannel touchpoint experiences. Keep in mind that beliefs and perceptions are often closely linked to cultural, gender and family influences and conditioning. Keeping ***relevant*** means operating a business receptive to continual learning as needed to deliver ***Durable*** customer value propositions. **Beliefs** drive customer buying habits that make your business's and your brand's *Competitive Advantage*. This is primarily communicated through ***Marketing*** and ***Customer Engagement*** practices that rely on message content and operational practices that:

- Satisfies customer brand preferences.

- Satisfies reasons to justify sustained customer brand loyalty.

To produce:

- Increased new customers and repeat sales.

- Longer total business and business model lifecycle longevity.

- Confidence in chosen business models.

Understanding and satisfying ***Belief-Alignment*** drivers is the starting point for the development of strategies to achieve continuous year-over-year customer satisfaction leading to and sustaining ***durability***.

Belief-Alignment (among customers, leaders, employees, partners and funding sources) is a characteristic among rapidly growing durable businesses. Belief-Alignment is a foundational element that needs to be part of a business's culture and team activities. People's beliefs influence how they function in a business. Believing in purpose, vision and mission drives behaviors that will encourage steps to make durability a reality. A collective belief system is a main trait that defines an organization's success.

Beliefs and visions put into practice is how you create durable value.

Beliefs drive behaviors that makes a business durable. They determine what you can do. Durability is the capability to translate beliefs into reality.

Elon Musk (Tesla Motors®, SpaceX®) believed that it is possible to create great accomplishments by changing the way things are done. He is the *Ultimate Futurist,* a big-picture visionary way beyond what most people might believe is science fiction. He clearly has the ability to translate beliefs into reality! He could not do this by himself. You might consider Elon Musk as the ultimate master of business *Belief-Alignment.* He is a true example of a person with leadership skills that solidify strategy and produce visionary applications and *Belief-Alignment* by:

- Having an expansive vision to see new realities.
- Building a customized path to reach his vision.
- Connecting with the necessary resources.
- Empowering a collaborative team (s) to complete required milestones.

Elon Musk's operational playbook and business purpose is clear. His businesses are making a real difference...he is creating a new reality.

A key initial task of every successful business is to determine how to relate to customer ***Beliefs***...as a core *Business Development* activity...in order to become and to remain year-over-year r***elevant***, r***esilient*** **and** d***urable***. This is not an easy task since everyone has personal beliefs derived from their numerous learnings and experiences. The task of great leaders is directing people in their business world (especially customers) to believe that their business solutions are their best option and that their workforce believes their business is a great place to work.

The most winning athletic coaches around the world are all experts in instilling a belief in winning as a fundamental attitude. The space program is a prime example of people collectively believing in a cause.

I call this possessing *Team-Centered Beliefs* (TCB), which just might be the most important driver of successful fast-growing businesses.

* * *

Continually pursuing awareness, insight and the understanding of Beliefs... customer/marketplace/ecosystem and organizationally...is a perpetual prospecting mode (PPM) that will help your business function better and give it a genuine, defensible Competitive Advantage.

How Wendy's® Disrupted McDonalds® and Burger King® by Promoting a Belief.

One of my favorite marketing campaigns was that of the fast-food chain Wendy's, the retail hamburger chain. In 1984 the market leaders in the fast-food burger industry were McDonald's and Burger King. These were two companies that used product names to position their products as large hamburgers (McDonald's Big Mac and Burger King's Whopper). Instead of following McDonald's and Burger King's marketing models, Wendy's chose a strategy to cast doubt on the actual size of their competitors' hamburgers; they were betting on the power of people's belief.

Wendy's developed the commercial catchphrase "Where's the Beef?" implying that their competitors' products were mostly buns. Wendy's even sold a square hamburger that protruded outside of their bun as a way to differentiate their product.

The "Where's the Beef?" campaign caught on quickly. Some say it is the most famous catchphrase ever. "Where's the Beef?" was quoted in political campaigns, in comedians' monologues and other forms of media presentations. It is memorable and sometimes used today.

Wendy's received awards from the advertising industry. But most of all, to the satisfaction of executives at Wendy's, sales increased significantly to propel Wendy's to the number three position in the fast-food industry at that time.

It is easy for a business to get mesmerized by short-term success, thus losing sight of longer-term goals such as durability. In this scenario, businesses can become strategically complacent as competitors create better competitive advantages. Yes, it is a dilemma since most compensation and award practices are based on short-term accomplishments.

For this reason, I encourage all members of a business's workforce (directly or indirectly connected to your business) to assist the C-suite leaders and the marketing department by continually monitoring the industry ecosystem for changes, challenges and opportunities. I call this operating in a PERPETUAL PROSPECTING MODE (PPM).

In 1969 Sears was the largest retail store in the world. In 2018 it filed for bankruptcy. Sears had historically grown by being very innovative, by changing strategies over time. At a point in time, trying new strategies was no longer part of its culture. Outdated operational practices eventually stifled growth and shrunk margins and profitability.

Sears lost sight of what was happening in the world around them. The company also strayed too far from its strengths in hard goods like tools and appliances. Discounting was being practiced by competitors such as Walmart and Target. Consumer buying preferences changed to included online buying. Budgets for store maintenance were ignored, hindering look and feel attributes.

Many scholarly articles have been written about the demise of Sears. They tell other aspects of the story. I like to focus on the marketplace influences. Even with some of the most well-known brand names (DieHard, Craftsman, Kenmore) the marketplace passed them by. Sears did not pay adequate attention to customer value proposition of the time. Sears became complacent following their legacy business models.

* * *

Relevancy and The Belief Alignment Process

The Number 1 reason businesses succeed or fail is their ability to become relevant…from a customer, buyer, user, organization perspective… and remain relevant over time.

To address the problem of *Relevancy*, I coined the ***Belief-Alignment*** concept…alignment between your business and the marketplace…as a customizable starting point for perpetual *Business Development to keep* strategies and tactics perpetually current and more precise. It should be practiced as a critical component of planning and tactical customer engagement reviews. ***Belief-Alignment*** evaluations can be easily performed by simply drawing a dividing line identifying which ***Beliefs*** will benefit your business and which will hamper your business. This type of educational insight and understanding can be sourced from research, customer engagement interactions, business trials or other places where market and industry ***Beliefs*** are evident. These ***Belief-Alignment*** reviews often produce results that initially seem contrary to planned business strategic direction. For this reason, ***Belief-Alignment*** activities need to be an endless part of a *Continuous Improvement* perpetual planning process such as the one included in this book *The Quest for Durability*.

There is no stronger priority for driving focused workforce behaviors than having a business embracing shared beliefs. It certainly is a message in every athletic coach's briefings. It drives collaboration to achieve goals. Every successful athletic coach knows this. People working together is how things get done.

Belief-Alignment just could be your business's most powerful competitive advantage. You may recall a highly publicized case in 1985 when Coca Cola® was losing market share. Coca-Cola ran some taste tests against Pepsi® and determined that people preferred the taste of Pepsi. To counteract this conclusion, they replaced their existing Coca-Cola formula with New Coke. However, this became a significant strategic mistake since the existing Coca-Cola customer base complained causing the Coca-Cola Company to withdraw New Coke and replace it with the previous Coca-Cola product they now called Coca-Cola Classic. Even though the marketing department of Coca-Cola felt that New Coke would be a better selling product than Pepsi, it did not happen.

The Strength of a Belief such as an Emotional Attachment Can Make a Difference

Coca-Cola is an international product selling belief based on a feeling good legacy (for about 100 years). Emotional feelings have always been a basic theme of their marketing campaigns. Brand loyalty embraced that theme. Consider some of their tag lines used in their branding programs:

- "Taste The Feeling."
- "Open Happiness."
- "I'd Like to Teach the World to Sing in Perfect Harmony."

The Coca-Cola Company learned that their market strength was not solely in their product...it was in customer beliefs and perceptions about the product brand that impacted customer loyalty, the true driver of their product sales.

Beliefs guide customer choices which satisfy your business's goal of obtaining lifecycle durable customer loyalty.

Always include the power of belief as a business model component for your business's long-term growth plans. Beliefs stimulate trust, product /service confidence, customer rapport and loyalty which generates repeat business producing repeat sales revenue.

Having relevant... tangible and intangible drivers...insight, understanding and foresight reinforces *Resiliency* and ultimately year-over-year business *Durability*. Achieving these objectives needs to be the result of multifaceted *Business Development review practices* focused on ensuring that customer *Beliefs* are compatible with your business's intended strategic solutions. ***Belief-Alignment*** is an imperative *Business Development* activity. Therefore, it is included as a starting point in this book.

Relevant Belief-Alignment simply stated:

RELEVANCY = BELIEFS AS SALES DRIVERS + BUSINESS STRATEGIC PLANS & TACTICAL ACTIONS

Beliefs originate from many different places. At this time, let's simplify the example by focusing on just two customer buying and purchasing influencers...price and emotions. They can't always be quantified, but they need to be understood.

Beliefs are not necessarily mutually exclusive. However, you can assume that people believe that their decision was the best thing to do to satisfy their preferences, needs, wants and desires. Highly successful companies know how to deliver a brand message that focuses on and reinforces these ***Beliefs***. The ongoing task to achieve ***Durability*** is building a feeling of confidence and emotional fulfillment in a buying decision, user adoption, or business transaction offered by your business.

As a result, clients, customers, users, employees, partners, investors and other supporters will engage with your business if they are aligned with what your business offers...e.g. the safest and/or best solution for their preferences, wants, needs, and desires.

Beliefs can be good or bad. For this reason, they need to be understood and managed accordingly.

What customers, buyers, users believe to be true or false will be the prime drivers of their purchase or no-purchase decisions, regardless of what your business leaders believe to be true.

* * *

BELIEF-ALIGNMENT AS A MARKETPLACE INFLUENCER

Understanding beliefs and belief mindsets *just may be the strongest influences on successful marketing programs.*

I have observed that customers are more likely to react favoring their **Beliefs** before considering specifics about product and service features and functions. For this reason, I recommend orienting brand messages and other marketing content around things people will mentally embrace. From a practical perspective, ***Belief-Alignment*** to a marketer is a practice of pairing ***Beliefs*** inherent to your *business* with those of your customers. Creating marketing strategies around ***Beliefs*** should be the foundation of successful message creation for branding programs. ***Beliefs*** have an extensive sphere of influence…all points of influence are important, such as:

- Preferences
- Behaviors
- Habits
- Likes and dislikes
- Experiences
- Attitudes

Implement Continual Prospecting (CP) practices appropriate for your industry to ensure your business has business models with resilient lifecycle longevity.

The qualitative and quantitative research are needed in order to truly understand and validate customer preferences, a constantly changing consideration differing depending on such things as customer demographics, target markets and technology capability influences.

More than ever, new ways of collecting data / information are evolving. For this reason, I encourage what I call *Continual Prospecting* (CP), drawing insight and understanding from such places as... technology-based capabilities, customer transactional tracking, and social media interactions.

The practice of including insight and understanding from *Continual Prospecting (CP)* sources, provides a visceral reaction and surfaces those emotional triggers, while follow-up surveys to a population sample provide metrics. Once they gather this information, successful marketers understand and know how to address these **Beliefs**...as reflected in their development of brand messages and other marketplace and organizational interactions and communications. Understanding ***Beliefs*** is also the knowledge base needed to allow for **perpetual strategic planning** needed to be successful in the future...it has a proven learning and growing application.

This matching process is important to establishing and maintaining *Brand* superiority and communicating organizational alignment of business purpose and vision.

Rapidly growing businesses have a habit of following ***Continuous Improvement*** practices to ensure that they have *insight* and *understanding* about ***Beliefs...***that can ultimately be effective to implement relevant, resilient and durable ***Belief-Alignment*** tested strategies and tactics.

This knowledge subsequently becomes main points of emphasis in their advertising and promotion programs and in the design of customer value proposition positioning.

Rapidly growing businesses put a significant amount of effort in the design of slogans which can be crafted to emphasize different themes such as...emotions, the benefits of doing business with your business, highlighting your business mission and creating recall of brand messages. These slogans helped their businesses obtain leading market share positions in their industries.

Examples of successful ***Belief-Alignment*** slogans...used to promote recall, confidence, trust and subsequent action:

- Wendy's®: Quality is our recipe
- Allstate®: You're in good hands
- Disneyland®: The happiest place on earth
- BMW®: The ultimate driving machine
- Subaru®: More than a car company

Researching and applying insight and knowledge about Beliefs influencing your marketplace, industry and your organization is a necessary step in strategic and tactical Business Development formulation needed to ensure that your business is following a path leading to growth, and defensible strategic substantiation.

BELIEFS as DRIVERS of BRAND REPUTATION

Businesses live and die based on their reputations.

I am sure you will agree...brand *reputation* is a formidable force influencing business performance. Credible reputations stimulate functions such as new sales, repeat business, brand loyalty, partnership arrangements and growth program implementation. Why is this important? Richard Branson said it best...

> *"Your brand is only as good as your reputation."*
> *—Richard Branson (Founder of the Virgin Group)*

Every business needs a strong *brand reputation to be a year-over-year Durable* business entity.

This means that prospecting for *Beliefs*...as needed to keep *Business Model(s) relevant*...needs to continually be part of a what I call a *Customer & Marketplace Expansion Process (CMEP)*...more about this in later chapters of this book. *The end result will be delivery of timely, flexible* strategic direction as needed reflecting the *Beliefs* of current and proposed target market audiences.

BELIEF-ALIGNMENT AS EVIDENCE–BASED SUBSTANTANTIATION

Nothing makes strategic and tactical rationale more believable than validated justification.

This book, *The Quest for Durability* includes a valuable synergistic, strategic and tactical planning tool I named *The Business Puzzle Method*™ approach...with its core eleven synergistic principles.

Following ***Belief-Alignment*** practices will strengthen the intent of *The Business Puzzle Method*™ approach...as a source of ***Evidence-Based Substantiation*** and what I call a ***Belief-Alignment*** function. They work together to substantiate strategies and tactics and to support compelling predictable outcomes.

When well analyzed and presented, ***Belief-Alignment*** points will have a powerful influence reinforcing *Risk Mitigation* justification and for the substantiation of major points needed to define your business's path to ***Durability***.

One of the main reasons that the USA space program has been successful is because people participating truly believe in the mission and everyone is willing to shoulder the task they were assigned. This allows multiple tasks at hand to collectively flourish...mission accomplished. It is visibly apparent...watch the cheers from program participants at every launch!

Belief satisfaction is basically a trust building strategy which increases workforce morale, encourages new business, repeat sales, and brand loyalty...not to mention the impact to a business's work environment. ***Beliefs*** are hard to change. However, if ***Beliefs*** are ignored and not considered as business priorities, business outcomes may very well miss their mark.

Beliefs should be ingrained principles that should never be compromised. Adherence to *Beliefs* enhance and attract customers and investors by proving that your business is worthy of their patronage and can be trusted. *Beliefs* reflect how a business is viewed by customers, influencing reputation and how a workforce views the world around them. There should never be a gap between what a business says their *beliefs* are and how they act.

Amazon has grown rapidly because customers believe they are the best answer to great customer service...convenience, fast delivery, product selection and a free shipping option. Customers believe this is their best purchasing option. Amazon understands the logic behind customer preferences. They deliver following continuous innovation practices... their main *competitive advantage*.

John Chambers, a past CEO of CISCO, in his book talks about changing people's perceptions about his company as a router manufacturer to a business with a bigger mission. He coined the phrase "The internet will change the way you work, live, learn, and play." His mission was to change the world with his company's products and services, not to sell routers. By the way, his mission was successful!

I predict, that for businesses to grow and survive in the future, they will have to emphasize ***Belief*** satisfaction brand messages that also support social responsibilities and environmental concerns, consistent with the ***Beliefs*** of their target markets... customers, investors, business partners, funding sources, social groups and employees. For these reasons, this book, *The Quest for Durability* rightfully starts with ensuring that *Business Plans* and corresponding *Business Models* verifiably match customer, marketplace and strategic requirements as a perpetual *prospecting, analysis and business model implementation requirement.* For example, companies like Tom's Shoes and Bombas socks that donate a pair for every pair purchased, Subaru's charity program for each car purchased—even Colgate is now producing recyclable toothpaste tubes.

It's not only true of upstart privately held companies. I anticipate seeing greater emphasis on softer issues (such as social and environmental impacts), when I read public company Form 10K reports from publicly traded companies (annual report required by Securities and Exchange Commission). These are customer preferences fast becoming influences on buying decisions.

Durability will increasingly require brand positioning with serious consideration for personal beliefs and values that line up with consumers' preferences.

Durability is More than Just Financial Success

The future of business durability must deal with more than profitability. Social and environmental concerns must be a durability imperative.

Programs need to have business models that also address social responsibilities and are environmentally conscious. More and more, social and environmental concerns will become important components of employment decisions and customer buying preferences based on contributing to social values. Concerns for our planet is a values-related manner vs the traditional financial perspective. Some major trends are leading the way:

- Automobile companies building electric vehicles.
- Recycled plastic products.
- Solar energy usage trends.

In the near-term and in the long run, marketing programs will need to include environmental and social considerations to build durable brand recognition, customer loyalty and to attract and retain a workforce. This rings especially true with the millennials and Gen-Z. Environmental and social programs will enhance a business's brand reputation which will serve to increase customer and employee satisfaction, partnerships and potentially satisfy the demands of funding sources and investors.

Identifying Beliefs ... internal and external to your business... adds insight, understanding and foresight needed to enable the development and execution of strategies and tactics focused on operating your business in a growth oriented, relevant, resilient, and durable way.

If you reread the ***Preface*** to this book, it addresses step one in the *Business Development* planning process...***Belief*** collaborations between businesses and customers. The following chapters will shift your attention to additional *Business Development* dimensions important to your overall planning and decision-making process...stimulating actions needed for success in this fast-changing competitive world.

Read on to develop your **perpetual blueprint** for your business... adopting *The Business Puzzle Method*™ approach...with rationale and compelling evidence-based components needed to be a year-over-year high-performing *Durable* predictable business.

The Power of Belief-Alignment

Business Development transformation is not just about delivering sales and service offerings, it is also about *why* the sales transaction occurred in a particular customer preference choice.

Keeping Mindsets Relevant

So, what are the influences that foster business durability? Simply stated, it starts with *Beliefs...which include perceptions, opinions and conversations...* the "Secret Sauce" as drivers of behaviors:

- You favor one business over another based on beliefs reinforcing confidence, trust, values and experiences.
- You make purchase decisions based on beliefs addressing such things as shopping preferences, quality and convenience.
- Your organization embraces a mindset of innovation because it *believes* in your vision, mission and purpose.
- You follow strategies based on beliefs that one strategy is better than another.

Continually pursuing awareness, insight and the understanding of Beliefs... customer/marketplace/ecosystem and organizationally...is a perpetual prospecting process (PPP) that will help your business function better and give it a genuine, defensible Competitive Advantage.

Chapter 2: Agile as a Strategy

(A Mindset, Culture And A Method For Business Lifecycle Durability)

Agile business practices constantly search for perpetual breakthrough innovation and resource collaboration as the foundational blueprint for relevancy, resiliency, business lifecycle longevity, value creation and year-over-year durability.

A business that is agile, from a strategic perspective, means a business with a shared purpose and vision that follows *Perpetual Planning* and *Continuous Improvement* (of core capabilities) practices that are flexible, adaptive, relevant, and timely as needed to build and maintain a business with DURABLE year-over-year lifecycle capabilities.

Following Agile as a Strategy (a mindset, culture alignment and a methodology) to augment the principles inherent in *The Quest for Durability / The Business Puzzle Method*™ approach by following *Perpetual Planning* and *Continuous Improvement* (of core capabilities) practices to be relevant, *stay resilient* and ultimately *be a durable business over time.* A further look as follows:

Transformational Components Driving Agility as a Strategic Practice:

- **Durability Focused Mindset (DFM):** to collectively embrace business purpose, vision, mission and goals.

- **Culture Alignment:** to encourage cross-functional collaboration and decision-making.

- **Methodology to Implement:** to facilitate collection of insight, determination of courses of action and to implement flexible, timely strategic direction.

Agility as a Strategy comes down to harnessing the power of teams and team thinking.

Attributes of an Agile Strategic Planning Environment

Being a lifecycle durable business means continually creating conditions that enables and accelerates profitable growth.

In a business that follows *Agile Strategic Planning* practices, every day is a day producing pivotal opportunities that could lead to *durability*. The following are conditions your business can create to stimulate transformative innovation.

- Focused purpose on both short-term and longer-term customer problem solving.

- Continuous thinking, strategizing, testing, validating and communicating.

- Collaborative development of transitional strategies and tactics of execution.

- Participation from all operational functions (internal and external).

- Shared critical insight, knowledge and understanding.

- Willingness to embrace business and marketplace shifting priorities.

- Culture aligned on business values, purpose, vision, mission and goals.

This is a dynamic approach to keep your business focused on what truly matters to be relevant, resilient and durable. Instead of operating with stagnant business plans, your business will have a PIPELINE of strategic options (such as keeping business models viable) compatible with your business's evolving strategic intent. As a minimum, agile strategic planning activities will:

- Stimulate feasible innovation.

- Reduce need for placeholder (short-term) strategic decision-making.

- Reduce concerns for risk-taking.

- Increase options for customer satisfaction.

- Focus business direction and activities on where you want to be in the future.

Durability is very much about continually determining in what industries your company wants to conduct business and then finding ways to perpetually make it happen.

ANOTHER NEED FOR FLEXIBILITY

An additional comment on this topic. Values should be consistent in all operations of a global business. However, always be aware of local customs and customer expectations. They can vary in different countries. For this reason, when I was in the international M&A business, I added the Country Manager, representing the region where I was working, to my planning and transition team. This ensured a good relevant cultural fit, so important to implementing *Agile Strategic Planning* practices.

AGILE THINKING AND ACTING (ATA)

An Agile Strategic planning orientation perpetually increases insight and understanding needed to keep your company's business models current and your business's path to goal attainment in prospective.

The more I study and experience the drivers of successful growth businesses, the more I am convinced that *Agility* is in the DNA in every fast-growing business. It is a business-wide operating mode of action that keeps a business creative and viable. I call this *Agile Thinking and Acting (ATA)*. From a strategic perspective, *Agile* (collaborative) thinking defines strategic development and execution practices, which should be part of your business's *Strategic Playbook*.

This Agile Strategic Playbook should combine strategy development and tactical execution determined from the Agile decision-making process.

Agile business development practices are a catalyst for new business and year-over-year durability.

This works well with *The Business Puzzle Method*™ approach principles of *Perpetual Planning* and *Continuous Improvement* practices. Agile strategic decisions need (development, testing, manufacturing) can be phased in over time. Agile as a Strategy allows for plan development and execution over time with continuous information feeds, a capability generally not part of traditional strategic planning processes.

Agile practices are best operated as continuous information / data collection and decision-making activity. This allows for continual decision-making with regard to assessing the need for various identified resources and for the redeployment of assets to higher needed programs as needed, making your strategic decisions more relevant and cost effective. A true benefit of Agile continuous planning and execution. Introducing proactive *Agile Strategic Thinking* could be the very thing your business needs to achieve and maintain a *Competitive Advantage.*

"When the rate of change inside an institution becomes slower than the rate of change outside, the end is in sight; the question is when."
—The late Chairman and CEO of General Electric® *Jack Welch*

Agile Thinking and Acting (ATA) needs to start at the strategy development stage of *Perpetual Planning* and also be reflected in *Continuous Improvement* initiatives. It is part of what I call having a *Durability Focused Mindset (DFM)* in a work environment of supportive relationships.

Agile Thinking and Acting (ATA) creates a baseline leading to lifecycle durability.

Agile Thinking and Acting (ATA), as a *Perpetual Planning* philosophy, is a Competitive Strength. It should have the flexibility to focus on market transitions in a timely manner.

From idea…to planned programs…to validated actions…to options for execution…to lifecycle updates.

Strategic planning is a necessity for all businesses. Not only do you need to plan for transitions for growth, but you also need to be prepared for market downturns and competitive pressures. *Agile* thinking keeps your functional teams focused on future outcomes. What makes a business durable is not its size. Even the largest of them sometimes fail. It is the ability to:

- Have a customer-centric focus throughout the business.
- Clearly communicate a compelling business purpose, vision and mission.

- Develop realistic and validated strategies, business models and tactics of execution.

- Understand customer current and future needs.

- Accelerate innovation ahead of the competition.

- Recruit and retain the correct talent and partners.

- Adopt new transformative technologies to continually improve productivity and performance.

- Be willing to refresh and reinvent strategies when necessary or when planned.

These strategic points are the essence of *Agile Strategy Thinking*. They need to be part of your business's Agile Strategic playbook. Keep them in mind when developing strategic direction since they will influence your business longevity.

Adding Agile practices to your strategic decision-making practices opens the gateway to your business's future.

Agile governance practices will increase chances to achieve sustainable success. This defines the capabilities of an *Agile* organization needed to define, implement and adjust *Strategic* and *Tactical* plans. The focus is timely decision-making utilizing all resources available to the business in a collaborative manner. An *Agile* organization is one that defines roles, priorities, and points of accountability and includes a measurement capability all leading to more effective *Decision-Making* and *Risk Mitigation*. An *Agile* mindset, operating within a collaborative organizational alignment is a best practice for facilitating an innovative culture as needed to be perpetually reinventing and transforming your business. It is the foundation for sustainable growth.

A business that has implemented Agile practices in functional organizations (in parts of or in total) demonstrates a willingness to accept change, a necessary ingredient to become a full lifecycle durable business entity. Companies that follow Agile practices can generally be identified by their ability to utilize various methods of prospecting (marketplace intelligence gathering), making frequent product/services changes within a collaborative functional organization. Include Netflix and Nike in this category.

The Power of Operating in an Agile Innovative Culture

To survive beyond a current timeframe, growth businesses need to operate in an Agile, innovative culture while planning to be a viable, year-over-year durable, profitable growth business in the mid to long-term time frames.

Let's define what we mean by an *Agile Management Philosophy:*

An Agile Management Philosophy is a principle of innovation and a mindset that is focused on dealing with real-time business issues needing flexible, fast decision-making actions. It operates in an environment of continual innovation, reinventing business processes as necessary, moving into new business space and introducing expanded and new customer solutions. This requires an organizational structure that can efficiently *reshuffle priorities* and *activities* when markets change, challenges arise and/or opportunities appear to perpetuate CONTINUITY...BUSINES PRACTICES FOR RESILIENCY.

PRACTICING INNOVATION IN TURBULENT TIMES

Operating in uncharted / unplanned market environments often requires revisiting purpose, priorities and operating model workflow practices.

As an example, one of the most impactful examples was The COVID - 19 global pandemic in 2020, which exemplified how quickly the marketplace can change. Nobody could have anticipated the global impact. Resiliency was disrupted. It was necessary to revise businesses models, rethink operations, reprioritize strategies and tactics and rearrange employee activities, partners in a purpose driven culture.

Pfizer, and other companies in the COVID – 19 vaccine development business could not have achieved vaccine development success without a focused agile development process. Pfizer created the first COVID –

19 vaccine in nine months. They created, tested and manufactured an end product so needed through the world. Clearly a business development success story to be applauded!

Pfizer set aside their standard development process for an agile business development methodology to expedite the creation and time-to-market delivery of the COVID – 19 vaccine. As stated by Dr. Albert Bourla (Chairman and CEO, Pfizer in his book (*Moonshot: Inside Pfizer's Nine-Month Race to Make the Impossible Possible*), they abandoned standard product development practices in favor of a fast time to market Agile team approach. They operated as a highly integrated, end to end operation, from early research to late-stage trials and clinical trials. They communicated in a seating arrangement of chairs called "The Purpose Circle" instead of at a table. Dr. Bourla developed Pfizer's streamlined R&D process. Their mission statement - "Breakthroughs that change patient's lives."

Yes, Pfizer implemented a best practice Agile business development process following what I call a *Just-in-Time Transition Planning (JITTP)* practice. The world is better off because of it.

Thank you, Pfizer.

THE BENEFITS OF PLANNING

There is no secret to achieving the benefits of planning, it is DURABILITY by design.

One of the benefits of Perpetual Planning is being prepared for both expected future and the unexpected future (regulatory compliance matters, natural disasters, and cyberattacks) and interruptions. This is another aspect of having what I call *Seamless Continuity Planning (SCP)* for building a path to your business's future. It is another output of *The Business Puzzle Method*™ approach to ensure Lifecycle endurance.

Much of the design and application of Seamless Continuity Planning (SCP) is industry specific. However, the goal in all industries is the same...it is resilience to maintain a degree of perceived risk and operational Durability while protecting a business's Competitive Advantage.

Addressing Agile Business Lifecycle Continuity Practices

Durability is not just about disaster recovery; it is about having seamless transitions from short-term to longer-term strategic direction.

As we have discussed, two of the main pillars of *The Business Puzzle Method*™ approach are Perpetual Planning and Continuous Improvement of core capabilities. Together they produce a capability to embrace change for BUSINESS LIFECYCLE CONTINUITY. This covers strategic planning for both planned and unplanned marketplace disruptions. Businesses with an understanding of their marketplace and industry have a handle on what is happening over a period on time and what can change. Operating in a business of Agile management will make your business Agile (flexible and adaptable) necessary to deliver timely marketplace solutions...typically called pivoting.

A business that follows Agile practices as a standard way of operating can MITIGATE disruptions per *The Business Puzzle Method*™ approach by focusing more easily on growth opportunities thus creating a new strategic definition of the business's "crown jewels." It is a transformation approach leading to *Business Lifecycle Continuity (BLC).*

* * *

Some Lifecycle Continuity Must-Haves:

- Synergistic short-term and longer-term purpose, vision, mission and goals.
- Seamless transitional strategies and tactics of execution.
- Master Plans for a growth trajectory.
- Always ready to redirect (pivot).
- Risk mitigating contingency plans.
- A positive brand reputation.
- On-going marketplace prospecting.

Agile business practices are a great way to keep your business relevant, resilient and ready to address the realities of your business's industry and marketplace.

DEFINING READINESS & CREDIBILITY LEADING TO DURABILITY

Following *Agile Management practices serves as* a *transformational catalyst* impacting leadership, governance and decision-making modes of operation. It operates in an environment of continual communication and feedback. Yes, this *mindset* often requires major operational reconfigurations, but it leads to increased "speed-to-market" for new and improved customer solutions.

* * *

WHEN AGILE BUSINESS DEVELOPMENT PRACTICES ARE NOT AN ADVANTAGE

Agile Management, as a business model, may not be appropriate for all functions of an organization or business. I recommend implementing *Agile Management* practices, or some degree of *Agile Management*, where major innovation is required to counteract rapid customer and marketplace change…to ensure *Business Model* and / or product/service *Lifecycle longevity*.

However, the entire business may not need to follow *Agile Management* practices. Some operations/business units within a larger business may be best operated as traditional hierarchical "siloed" operations, especially if the main focus of the organization is as a "cash-cow" (e.g. business jargon for a business that is a slow grower or not growing at all but producing more than adequate cash flow) that can be channeled to faster growing areas of your business. This may be best accomplished by following legacy methodologies and embedded capabilities. A business or business unit being prepared as part of a divestment strategy probably should follow legacy practices demonstrating stability. When to use *Agile* Management practices, and the extent of usage, should be looked at on a situation-by-situation basis.

Encourage Focusing on Transformational Perpetual Planning and Continuous Improvement informational sources

Achieving business durability requires a constant learning experience.

Experience demonstrates that durability happens when your business organization is focused on both *strategy formulation* and *corresponding execution*. Strategic decision-making should be included as an organizational real-time, all-inclusive activity in a business. New *market intelligence* and *insights* surface when the environment is receptive to listening and acting appropriately.

This requires migrating from a business that primarily spends its time taking care of day-to-day transactions, without taking notes on the good points and the not so good points around how transactions are handled. Business employees, suppliers and partners, etc. need to function with what I call a ***Durability Focused Mindset (DFM)***, constantly asking the questions needed to determine and prioritize transitional strategic direction.

*Following **Perpetual Planning** and **Continuous Improvement** practices allows for the ability to pursue a path to durability as an **evolutionary practice**, instead of a reactionary activity needing implementation before it is too late.*

Enable Roll-Out of Transition Programs as You Need Them

I have always been a believer in planning and doing constructive things to influence your own destiny. This is also a key philosophy when operating a business with an intended purpose to be *durable*. To make this happen, it generally takes a change in thinking, actions and accountability. This is having a ***Durability Focused Mindset (DFM)***. This mode of thinking (including agile ways of thinking where applicable) encourages a unifying process that supports an end-to-end strategic planning process through a durable tactical lifecycle of mission achievement, customer satisfaction and monetary returns.

Following *The Business Puzzle Method*™ approach will make it possible to disrupt the marketplace (or enhance your business models) on your terms in a timeframe of your choosing. It is an innovation origination and management process that brings together synergistic requirements to operate your business as a year-over-year *relevant, resilient* and *durable* business entity. Implement your business's growth programs on your own terms in your own timeframe.

Avoid the Hazard of Procrastination

Perpetual Planning is the remedy for procrastination and the solution to be a relevant, resilient, and durable business entity. It is the source of the development of continual transformation considerations.

The most frequent deterrent to operational change that I have witnessed is what I call *Decision Procrastination (DP).* Procrastination generally leads a business to eventually needing to fight for survival and/or heading towards extinction. The marketplace does not wait for anyone!

I have frequently experienced businesses that have a tendency to *procrastinate* when it comes to changing business direction (pivoting). They are mesmerized with current performance and/or have internal strong feelings that they have a lasting business model. *Procrastination* and *business stagnation* can emanate from within a business as well as from marketplace pressures. In this profoundly and rapidly changing world, there are numerous reasons why a business justifies why their business model status quo is the chosen path to follow. Just look at Sears, Blockbuster and Kodak...classic examples of *procrastination* in *decision-making*. A durable business needs to constantly reset itself to meet a host of challenges while simultaneously addressing opportunities.

An Agile Management Philosophy influences actions, dialogue and practices stimulating innovation which is fundamentally the act(s) of creating value by being relevant, resilient and durable.

Agile Team Philosophy Summarized

Agile teams are the heart of the Agile Management Philosophy...most effective when collaborative insight is embedded in both the planning decision-making process and the day-to-day operations of a business.

Businesses are stronger when operating as cross-functional teams. They create momentum and deliver skills capabilities beyond those of individuals.

Agile Teams are a Lifecycle Durability Enabler (LDE)

People resources (when properly organized and motivated) are what I call a ***Lifecycle Durability Enabler (LDE)***. People resources have the greatest impact when deployed as an ***Agile Team***.

People are typically a business's most important asset. This in itself is a challenge. People include a variety of leadership and decision-making styles, a mix of capabilities and degrees of commitment levels. What makes this an even more challenging situation is that requirements for people resources is not a constant. Requirements change as the landscape and ecosystem changes causing gaps in the ability to hold or expand market share and create a *durable* future...a significant consequence of reality!

Team Dynamics Need to Be Durable

The greatest challenges of any size business are keeping up with changing customer expectations, addressing evolving opportunities needed to grow the business while servicing an existing and/or new expanded customer base. *Durability requires creating innovative strategies that deliver tactical marketplace engagement solutions.*

For the fastest growing businesses I observed, this is best performed as a **TEAM** event based on four fundamental pillars:

1. People with a *Durability Focused Mindset (DFM).*
2. A business operating in a culture receptive to change & encouraging innovation.
3. Teams aware of marketplace & landscape realities around them.
4. A desire to address realities and grow a profitable, durable business.

In summary, *Agile Teams* are adaptive "Agents of Change." They have to constantly be learning. Their spheres of influence need ingenuity to be creative, flexible, resourceful and timely as their role in a business enters subsequent stages of development. The role of *Agile Teams* is to create more value for the business, customers, partners and other stakeholders. This is an organizational design imperative to perpetuate strategies and tactics needed for year-over-year durability.

In my more than a decade as the Executive Director of the iconic Enterprise Development Center (EDC, renamed VentureLink) at New Jersey Institute of Technology (NJIT), it became clear to me that businesses following Agile business values and practices were the ones destined to succeed the fastest. Founders and CEOs hired people who complemented their skills and experiences, operated in a collaborative manner and functioned within a collaborative network. This makes a lot of sense since any business in a formative and/or expansion stage needs to be receptive and flexible to new ideas and ways to get things done. They operated the best by being in the mode of listening and learning.

As I have stated previously, all successful businesses need to always have new or rejuvenated business models in their pipeline to be relevant, resilient and durable. Fast growing businesses usually accomplish this by following Agile business development practices, whether it be in the management of product / service development, research, manufacturing, marketing and sales, supply chain or backroom administrative activities. My observation is that the extent of Agile practices is not uniformly applicable to all parts of a business but when applied must deliver *Perpetual Planning* advice and *Continuous Improvement* initiatives. The adoption of Agile business practices represents a paradigm shift that will significantly influence businesses of the future.

Large businesses are adapting Agile Management practices (especially in the business development areas) to advance innovation and improve efficiency. It all comes down to encouraging flexible, creative leadership to advance transformational change.

One of my favorite examples is demonstrated by the leadership style of Elon Musk...founder of SpaceX and CEO of Tesla Motors. He is what I call a *Change Focused Leader (CFL)*. His style is to encourage *Agile* team innovation vs traditional CEOs who are mesmerized by income statements and balance sheets. Elon Musk is a proven example of someone who is flexible and resilient.

Agile organizations are quick to drive innovation and adapt to change.

SpaceX is considered by many as an Agile company. They have invented new ways to rapidly move manufacturing from design to test in expedited time. They operate with Cross-functional teams to expedite progress, have Agile innovation and operate within an Agile decision-making process. Agile business development practices are a form of *Perpetual Planning* combined with initiatives derived from *Continuous Improvement.*

"Innovation often doesn't come through one breakthrough idea, but through a relentless focus on continuous improvement"—Elon Musk

To be a lifecycle durable business in the future, it is critically important to determine which portions of your business will require Agile innovation and reinvigorating...as a business development priority.

***Agile Teams* need to collectively and continuously master such things as:**

- Purpose, vision, mission and goal.
- Customer and market requirement.
- Organizational alignment to encourage innovation.
- People, know-how and understanding.
- Technology capabilities.
- Focused brand identity in target markets.
- Channels to be utilized.
- Evaluated and prioritizing courses of action.
- Financial requirements and return expectations.

Agile Teams make extraordinary businesses happen! The quest for Durability is a never-ending journey. Collaborative *Agile Team* actions will bring your business to a higher level of relevant, resilient success.

Continual Strategic and Tactical Positioning and Repositioning to Become and to Remain Durable

People and networks, internal and external to your business, should be a major source of the real-world assumption development defining the logic of proposed strategies and tactical positioning. The better the communication among teams the greater the advantage in your *decision-making* process.

People knowledge should not be ignored. Ideas can originate from any part of your business (internal & external). Team insight should continually be augmented by new technologies where applicable.

Fortune 500 Companies (for example Cisco, IBM) are increasingly adopting agile practices to accelerate "speed to market" of products and services. Industry changes due to the rapid introduction of new technologies is a primary cause. Smaller businesses have migrated to Cloud for file storage, sharing and backup capabilities. Resident businesses at the EDC at NJIT used to have racks of hardware in their offices to perform development and customer services. Today they employ a more flexible, agile approach by utilizing cloud services to accelerate development of their strategic capabilities.

I call this continual refinement process as ***Perpetual Prospecting (PP),*** an important input component of *strategic* and *tactical* plan preparation. Perpetual Prospecting (PP) draws knowledge from all parts of the business as input to the decision-making process...clearly an Agile practice.

Agile Teams are composed of like-minded multidisciplinary members who have a specific task to accomplish and are willing to share their knowledge. More likely than not, ***Agile Teams*** are more flexible than those in traditional "Silo" (business term favoring organizationally separated operations and decision making) operations. They can understand and respond to change and challenges in a timelier manner.

The problem with a business and organizations that operates with a Silo management model is that these practices have a tendency to exclude input from many people associated with business operations and in decision-making.

THE SKUNK WORKS® TEAM STORY

I consider businesses that operate within a *Siloed* management model as having leadership behaviors detrimental to the durability of their business. I first was exposed to the concept of *Agile* management after reading about one of the first implementations of what I call *counter-silo* practices, implemented at Lockheed® Aircraft Corporation in 1943 during World War II. At that time, jet aircraft needed to be developed in an extremely short time. To accommodate this task, Lockheed put together secretive teams of engineers who were separate from the rest of the company which was focused on manufacturing current generation aircraft. Today we refer to such practices as "intrapreneurship." These empowered teams had the authority to operate as independently as needed to accomplish their goals (building state-of-the art aircraft in the shortest time possible.) They operated outside of the mainstream business following a self-managed operating model focused on disruptive innovation. The result was development of much needed jet aircraft (jets were not in use by the USA at that time in World War II) and subsequent later developments.

- P-80 Shooting Star jet in 143 days.
- U-2, the world's first spy plane.
- SR-71Blackbird, capable of reaching a speed of Mach 3 (the fastest and highest-flying aircraft at that time).

I am sure there are many other great disruptive accomplishments completed by the Skunk Works® engineers. What impressed me as a student of management practices was **HOW** the Skunk Works® engineers operated. They were operating with complete control in a collaborative manner, accomplishing goals in record time. The Skunk

Works® operating practices was the proving ground of what we call *Agile* business practices today.

Note: The name Skunk Works® was adopted from a popular newspaper comic strip, "Li'l Abner."

The ***Agile Team*** *approach is best suited for situations where speed-to-market, speed-to-design, speed-to manufacturing and speed-to-implementation is critical according to common milestones.*

The biggest disadvantage to Silos (defined as functional organizations favoring their own organizational interests) is a tendency to resist change. In addition, they usually produce conflicts when determining budget and other resource allocations.

In my M&A due diligence days, I could immediately spot businesses that are functioning in a Silo world. Department reviews produced disjointed statements of strategy and business milestones. Sometimes business Executive Summaries did not match the Business Plan or sub-plans. In addition, employees were not willing to support the position of other departments. In these cases, there is no continuity of priorities and milestones. These situations reflect GAPS that influence business strategic viability and valuation.

To be a year-over-year durable business, your business's planning activities need to synergistically reinforce or produce new business models to keep your business on a continual growth trajectory. I call this building **Transformational** ***Business Models (TBM)...*** appropriate for your specific business and industry at a specific point in time (now or in the future). This is best accomplished via an ***Agile Team*** aligned on a common business purpose, with a view for the future to make it happen. **Durability** requires **Agile Teams** from multiple departments working together to transform a business.

Successful ***lifecycle durable business development*** conclusions move at the pace that visionaries see change and identify new opportunities. Rapidly growing businesses become a dominant marketplace force by following methodically orchestrated strategic planning and follow-up tactical execution programs which are included in the framework of ***The***

Business Puzzle Method™ approach. It is cooperative Agile Team activities that best produce lasting performance excellence and competitive advantages. It is how innovation happens.

Chapter 3: A Great Idea is Not Enough

(The need for commercially viable solutions)

Ideas are abundant, what is needed is a methodology to make them into a durable business model.

Success is best achieved by establishing a realistic vision, mission and collaborative purpose, by operating in a culture of co-created innovation, by developing strategies with executable tactics, by being focused on customer-facing solutions all justified based on synergistic evidence and analysis.

One of my most important realizations driving the philosophy behind this book is the awareness that everything (technology and life science based) we experience today was at onetime someone's vision. How that vision advanced from an idea to a business model and product/service solution is the formula for *business lifecycle durability*.

- Thomas Edison invented the light bulb. That in itself was an accomplishment but how electric light service reached households is a story of true innovation.

- Curing polio was a vision of Dr. Jonas Salk. He was successful in developing a polio vaccine, one of the most significant biomedical advances at that time.

- Clarence Birdseye's idea to flash freeze food.

BIRDS EYE

One of my favorite innovation stories is about the invention of 3M brand Post-it Notes®.

They are small (originally) note papers with sticky backs that are today used by just about everyone. It was invented by a chemist who specialized in adhesives technology at 3M Central Research Labs. What especially interests me is the fact that Post-it-Notes was a product of failed experiments intended to make extra strong adhesives. It is a product with low adhesive capabilities that could be removed and reused. 3M initially had no interest in such a product. It was viewed as having no market.

Some years later, a fellow 3M chemical engineer (in 3M's tape division) heard of the low adhesion glue. He needed to replace the bookmarks he used in his hymnbook. He applied the low adhesive glue to small strips of paper and made bookmarks. Yes, a new application…originating from a failed adhesive development program that had the intent of developing a super strong glue.

I see 3M's Post-It Note's story as an example of the need to bring together idea creativity, innovation, and decision making. The product / service solution is not always initially obvious, in fact it could be an accidental revelation!

In reality, they had invented a new way to be organized and to communicate. The story goes that 3M used canary yellow paper because it was scrap paper available at the time. Today, product extensions (colors, sizes, applications) are a testimonial to the popularity of 3M's Post-It Note.

3M's Post-it Note was a product that nobody originally thought had a commercial market. In fact, original test markets (in 1977) did not produce encouraging results. However, its characteristic (of NOT being a product that permanently adheres) has a huge commercial following and customer loyalty. Quite a revelation for 3M, a company famous for creating strong adhesives.

Finding a way to develop and implement a vision is what makes the world of solutions possible. *The Business Puzzle Method*™ approach is such a process.

So often, (especially while serving as the Executive Director of the iconic Enterprise Development Center (EDC) at New Jersey Institute of Technology (NJIT), I have been presented with very imaginative ideas. (The EDC worked primarily with startup and expansion businesses.) Most likely it was an app or some other kind of product or service offering. Certainly, this is a start of a business model idea. The challenge this coach had was getting the business's CEO (and his/her team) to focus on:

- The depiction of the idea as a business, not just a technology.

- Assembling a total business plan / view of how the idea will be developed, manufactured, sold, serviced and supported by their organization to create a sustainable business model leading to a competitive advantage.

- Developing a VALIDATED customer value proposition around the idea.

- Focused on the customer perceived value and benefits vs the features and functional capabilities of the idea.

An idea without a blueprint (Business Plan) and a clearly defined path for launch and maintaining operations will not succeed. A business transition framework is needed (as is included in *The Business Puzzle Method*™ approach) for strategic creation and tactical execution of an idea. This book will touch on some of the most needed embedded synergistic aspects:

- To develop compelling strategies with executable tactics.
- To have relevant, resilient short-term & longer-term continuity as a growth priority.
- To operate in a culture of innovation and value-added thinking.
- To define how your business will execute business plans, operate and bring in a monetary return.
- To establish key tracking activities and dependencies.
- To maintain a strong brand presence with a loyal, trusting following.
- To operate with relevant, resilient customer engagement practices.
- To prepare for possible pitfalls with courses of correction.

In summary, a business idea must bring value to your customers, value to your business and partners (operationally and financially), while adding to your business's competitive advantage and lifecycle durability.

Lifecycle Durability is about developing a realistic plan and focusing day-to-day activities on living that plan.

Moving Beyond a Short-Term Business Continuity Survival Plan

Looking into the future, the pursuit of durable innovation will require creativity, flexibility, resilience, timing and a purpose beyond a current snapshot in time.

Looking Into the Future – A Business Development Lifecycle Longevity Approach

In these uncertain times, it is important to find new ways "to stay the course" and build new paths for individuals, communities, government and business resilience. The new norm has yet to be defined and may continually change. The underlying principles of most business models are being challenged. It is no longer possible to rely on legacy business models. Therefore, paths for future resilient business continuity will need strategies and tactics with a focus on long-term sustainable, profitable growth.

Business Model Scenario Planning – Strategic Alignment for the Future

Once a degree of short-term business continuity has been reached, it is now time to think even further into the future. Many actions enacted during the pandemic era may not be ideal and/or sustainable into the developing marketplace that will follow. In addition, new opportunities may now appear possible that were not previously considered in your thought process. In reality, a crisis such as the pandemic is just another stimulation for innovation. It is time for business model review and the creation of new and/or improved strategy, tactics and tactical implementation programs to also reach long-term sustainable profitable growth.

Addressing an Innovative Planning Model – Change on an Accelerated Timetable

The most innovative companies (e.g. Amazon®, Apple®) always have new or improved strategic plans (in the form of disruptive products/services) on the drawing board. There is no reason a smaller company can't embrace a similar planning philosophy on a smaller scale. Start by completing an inventory of strengths, weaknesses and realistic business model actions needed to sustain a realistic Business Continuity position. Then implement a philosophy embracing continual planning for the future to produce a path to surpass and/or supplement anticipated performance outcomes and prepare to address the opportunities and challenges of the future.

Rethinking Business Model Intent and Scope – Develop Initiatives for Sustainable, Profitable Growth

* * *

Things to do for Business Lifecycle Longevity and Continuity

Durability is about obtaining the transformable insight and foresight needed to formulate seamless short-term and longer-term seamless continuity strategies and the ability to execute lasting customer preferred business models.

Building a business model (with sustaining power) requires the intent of possibly a new or revised core vision/mission determined during a previous Business Continuity development process.

Maneuvering (e.g. pivoting) requires long term strategic planning. It is critical to plan for and be prepared to meet a new norm, whatever that is. Sustainable, profitable growth is the longer-term objective.

Change tactical execution of current business practices to meet evolving market demands.

I have listed but not elaborated on these points for the sake of communication brevity. I will not go into the details at this time. However, it is my hope that these points will allow your business to quickly focus on what is most important for your specific business.

Some ideas to consider:

- Improve performance of working capital (inventory, accounts receivable, accounts payable).
- Evaluate continual ability to deliver customer value proposition.
- Implement new or continue employee remote access capabilities.
- Negotiate more favorable business agreement terms.
- Move to e-commerce sales/service ordering.
- Utilize video conferencing as a communication solution.
- Change revenue billing formula from one-time billing to recurring charges or payment plans.
- Reduce general and administrative costs.
- Reduce and/or share workforce and workload responsibilities.
- Offer financial assistance to customers.
- Renegotiate and/or waive fees and payment requirements.
- Transfer selective capabilities to cloud-based suites.
- Partner with communities for collaborative relationships.

I developed these points based on my notes from my experiences. They are just some ways to generate business momentum…to sharpen a focus on organizing, planning and prioritizing to achieve performance durability goals. How they can be utilized in your individual business plans is the task of a *Perpetual Planning decision-making process* appropriate for your industry and business growth stage.

Update vision, mission goals for revised or a new definition of customer value.

The trend towards globalization is indicative of businesses that demonstrate adaptability. McDonalds® (the foodservice retailer) has menus adapted for many different countries to adapt to their preferences in menu options and dining habits.

I remember being in China visiting the Forbidden City (no longer forbidden) in Beijing. I noticed a McDonalds sign not too far away. My party and I decided to visit the McDonalds to experience the marketing approach in China. What we found was not a fast-food restaurant but instead a sit-down restaurant that also served Chinese dishes. It is a flexible strategy that is working. There are more than 3 thousand McDonalds in China. I found that adopting local menus was a strategy followed by McDonalds all over the world. Other restaurants have followed the same strategy.

Business model flexibility is clearly a strategy driving global growth for many businesses. Being adaptable is a key to business growth and yes, timing is everything.

MORE ABOUT THINGS TO DO FOR BUSINESS LIFECYCLE CONTIUITY

A Continual Future Needs Alignment (CFNA) to be Performance Predictable and Durable.

Strategic plans should not be a snapshot in time at a particular date but instead should be the result of perpetual plans (plus continuous

improvement of core capabilities) frequently modified and updated to address current and future change, challenges and opportunities.

The path to durability is about delivering over time the needed solutions that are most important to customers. **Durability** is not about selling product and service features and capabilities. It is about having the perspective of satisfying customer needs, wants, desires and preferences which will change as industries and customer preferences evolve. It is about developing business models that serve a greater purpose of delivering needed benefits to customers, however configured.

This requires a continual planning process featuring timely, flexible capabilities addressing the challenges and opportunities which I call **CONTINUAL FUTURE NEEDS ALIGNMENT (CFNA)**, a key capability possible by following *The Business Puzzle Method*™ approach.

I call this planning output as the "**Show Me**" proof of relevancy, resiliency and durability...

Referring back to my example of the Shark Tank question as to why the contestants think their business has such a high valuation, it can be answered by presenting rationale and logic based on the insight and knowledge prepared by following *The Business Puzzle Method*™ approach. One of the major benefits of following *The Quest for Durability* / The Business Puzzle Method™ approach is the preparation of *Evidence-Based Substantiation (EBS).*

Evidence-Based Substantiation (EBS) produces an enhanced persuasion capability so critically important to rationalizing business needs, growth strategies and tactics of all kinds. Follow a path to produce a strategic, tactical and organizational capability to produce a ***Blueprint for Strategic and Tactical Success (BSTS)*** in order to defend the logic required to substantiate ***Performance Predictable*** outcomes.

Nothing beats substantiated logic, facts and figures to de-risk a business and strengthen a negotiation position.

Change Business Model

Always-ready - Perpetual planning for growth needs to be a critical-mission of your business. Durability is about *setting the Course for the Future and being Always-Ready* for change, challenges, interruptions and opportunities. Being *Always-Ready* (a key success factor) means that *timing* is critical in any game plan where the execution of strategies and tactics needed for your business to be relevant, resilient and durable. Being prepared allows your business to implement disruptive marketplace actions or react to disruptive competitive actions.

IBM, a business that historically was an industry leader in computers abandoned the hardware business in the 1990's to refocus on software, consulting services. Subsequently they split the company into two pieces... one that delivered cloud computing artificial intelligence and another that focused on IT services.

NETFLIX moved from a company that rented DVDs to a streaming entertainment provider. Cisco moved from a one product business (routers) to a giant tech company with products that are the backbone of the internet. These companies were ***Always–Ready*** to meet the changing needs of the world.

Deciding what your company should strategically do next is a result of Perpetual Planning learnings, a necessary capability to continually be a market leader.

I recall the story of the man running on the train platform who ultimately missed his train. Another person said, "You need to run faster." He responded by saying, "No, I needed to have left earlier." This is the essence of *Perpetual Planning and Continuous Improvem*ent... anticipating change, challenges and opportunities and reacting on your terms as you visualized them.

This is best done by planning to be prepared and updated continuously over business lifecycles:

- Adjusting your vision, mission and goals to address evolving customer/marketplace expansion opportunities.
- Building on your business's strengths.
- Creating lasting brand recognition and customer loyalty.
- Providing seamless short-term and long-term customer experiences.
- Drawing on your collective business and network expertise and know-how.
- Substantiating rationale for lines of credit and growth program financing.

This seems to be obvious but not always followed. Look at the demise of Sears, Kodak, Blockbuster, Wang Labs, Digital Equipment and other businesses often studied as business failures. Sure, there were multiple reasons why they failed. However, the one common reason was not having a timely, innovative ***Redirect*** (pivoting) strategy leading to a different kind of viable future. This intriguing business phenomenon continues to persist and provides an important lesson.

Successful businesses have learned to differentiate themselves from unsuccessful businesses by following *Perpetual Planning* and core *Continuous Improvement (of on-going business practices)* business development practices as included in *The Business Puzzle Method*™ approach. I term this having a **Durability Focused Mindset**.

* * *

FOUNDATION for VALUE-CREATING PHILOSOPHIES and PRACTICES

Business growth and relevant, resilient and durable solutions are made up of multiple piece parts (or puzzle pieces), each of which has influence on your business's viability and overall ability to succeed.

When the piece parts are viewed together, they complement and synergistically present powerful logic for strategic and tactical plan formation and execution. *The Business Puzzle Method*™ approach presents a clear view and a business development consciousness…to satisfy multiple constituents (i.e. customers, management, employees, suppliers, boards, stockholders, funding sources, investors). *The Business Puzzle Method*™ approach is an innovative managerial way to develop insight and understanding, evaluate and present your business plan strategies and tactics in the marketplace and in the business community. This is accomplished by implementing a practice of doing business (*The Business Puzzle Method*™ approach) that features the sharing of synergistic influences as a source of year-over-year relevancy, resiliency and durability. It is a methodology that encourages expanding your business based on those things that influence the rationale for substantiated strategies and tactics vs the historical fixation on profits or numeric measures.

SOME ESSENTIAL PHILOSOPHIES AND PRACTICES

Lifecycle durability is not the outcome of coincidences and lucky breaks. Lifecycle durability requires a strategic approach to accelerate growth as needed to ensure that the business does not get stuck in stagnation, or worse yet—a downward trajectory.

The Quest for Durability and *The Business Puzzle Method*™ approach identify factors that when followed will take your business into a mode of operation sustaining *lifecycle longevity and year-over-year durability*.

Must-Haves In Order To Be a Lifecycle Durable Business:

- Actionable Perpetual Planning and core Continuous Improvements to deal with year-over-year insight, foresight and to improve decision-making.

- Always-Ready flexible, timely business model Migration Plans and backup Contingency Plans to deal with life cycle longevity matters, landscape changes and achievement of growth goals.

- Creative Innovative Culture with an Innovative Mindset operating following collaborative governance practices.

- Continual prospecting to understand relevant customer needs, desires and preferences.

- Seamless Short-Term to Longer-Term Continuity plans.

- Validated operational and financial Performance Outcome Predictability.

- Feasible Risk Mitigation programs.

* * *

Chapter 4 Planning for Success
(Capturing The Key Lifecycle Durability Influences)

TRANSFORMATION OF STRATEGIC AND TACTICAL PRIORITIES

The Problem:

Many businesses place too much emphasis on their legacy business practices to include "siloed" cultures defining their decision-making practices. They more than likely have their people resources and practices slanted towards handling day-to-day customer needs as their highest priority. This is very understandable but not a long-term *durable* business practice.

Back in my days in a market management organization, we received a considerable number of complaints from customers who were being serviced by a particular call center. Upon further review, we learned that the complaints were driven by a call center measurement practice that required the call center operators to terminate a customer call after a specified period of time, regardless of the status of the caller's resolution.

This practice was explained by the call center management team as a labor-saving strategy that could be measured in less staffing and overtime requirements. While the call center had good intentions, this was a legacy business practice that needed to be changed. They ignored the real purpose of their job which was customer satisfaction, which was needed to encourage customer loyalty and repeat business.

This is not an uncommon type of scenario. When I see similar business practices, I can predict the longevity of the business and conclude…it is a business NOT focused on relevant, resilient, and durable strategic transformation practices.

Transformation strategies often requires significant changes in core business ideologies, specifically core purpose and goals. As in the example previously cited, movement to *lifecycle durability* practices in itself can be a disrupter. Moving away from legacy business practices and siloed decision-making to include the practice of thinking that profits are not the sole purpose of a business (a concept counter to those businesses that are evaluated by Wall Street leaning people).

Lifecycle Durability is about being willing to adapt in a timely manner in a rapidly changing world and/or be willing to drive the changes according to plans.

LEADING CHANGE REQUIRES PREPARATION

The Solution:

The solution to operating as a business following short-term practices is corrected by following *Innovative Planning and by Managing Risks.*

The central ideas to make lifecycle durability a priority - simply stated:

- Defining targeted durable outcomes.
- Pursuing critical activities / milestones to achieve justifiable outcomes.
- Understanding challenges & opportunities anticipated.
- Measuring growth trajectory, outcome progress & modifying as required.

Lifecycle Planning is about preparation and disciplined execution of reinforcing, synergistic capabilities—not on any single capability alone.

Growth trajectories require that a successful *durable* business must always be in some state of transition. *Perpetual Planning* and *Continuous*

Improvement of core capabilities will allow for your business to drive change, not just react to the competition. This makes total sense since your business (to be durable) must operate in a world that never stops changing.

When all is said and done, business is still conducted and led by *people* that run companies. Therefore, any business is only as successful as its leadership in all functional organizations—and its leadership must learn to embrace durability.

Leadership Priorities to be Durable.

Forward-looking strategic planning leadership teams (in all job functions of the organization) should constantly be looking for ways to achieve and maintain a Competitive Advantage.

One thing that has always resonated with me is that all successful businesses were once startups. It makes sense to study and emulate, were appropriate, their learnings and follow their examples (successes and failures).

THE COMMON CHARACTERISTICS FOR A DURABLE COMPETITIVE ADVANTAGE

Successful businesses have found a way to leverage *Insights, foresight, understanding* and capabilities by modifying cultural norms, changing operating practices and implementing business strategies that can deal with realities and deliver targeted outcomes over time.

Your business's future will require many new beginnings influenced by perpetual learnings, proactive initiatives and validation experiences.

One of the principles in *The Business Puzzle Method*™ approach is that successful businesses are businesses constantly in a change mode…to grow and adapt to the surrounding world viewed as opportunities and organize your business around addressing them. Durability is about how your business responds to change, challenges and opportunities and being a business willing to move from current strategic "comfort zones."

Innovation priority initiatives mean different things to different businesses

There is no "one size fits all" definition for transitional strategic planning. Innovation strategies depend on the size and maturity of your business.

Businesses run by founders generally succeed by following these entrepreneurial practices. Small businesses can leverage C suite and functional organization leadership through direct interaction. Their vision and leadership made them what they are today. The Walt Disney Company is what it is today because of Walt Disney's influence on his business's vision, mission, strategies and practices. Business literature is full of such stories.

In my experience, I have worked with CEOs whose only desire is to innovate startup and early-stage businesses and functional line managers who only want to work on new or improved products and services. They do not want to operate mature businesses. In addition, they want to primarily grow their businesses via organic (revenue from existing or modified business models and existing operational capabilities) sales methods.

Long-term durability generally requires a continual change or addition of people resources to reach multiple growth milestones. Without this, businesses become stagnant. Having a vision and a plan demands the right resources to develop and execute the plan during the appropriate timeframe. Plans need the appropriate people capabilities to be relevant, resilient and durable over time consistent with lifecycle transition strategies.

People capabilities in your business must keep pace with visions and missions otherwise growth plans are no more than dreams.

* * *

DURABILITY BY FOLLOWING HYBRID ORGANIC AND INORGANIC STRATEGIES

For larger more mature businesses, there is usually a different approach to delivering targeted durable outcomes over time. They typically do things differently by combining organic and inorganic (mergers, acquisitions, joint ventures) to their business expansion programs. Look at Apple; they frequently add to their mobile phone offerings while concurrently engaging in M&A activities.

TYPICAL BUSINESS EXPANSION STRATEGIES

Successful durable businesses require a combination of practices and disciplines leveraging existing and transitional behaviors, capabilities and actions.

A sampling of my favorite proven expansion strategies:

- Replace internal product development with acquisitions of small lean startups.

- Initiate Joint Ventures.

- Merge with other established businesses.

- Build industry partnerships.

- Licensing of technology.

- Divest poorly contributing business units / operational components for cash creation.

For example, Brunswick Corp. divested business units that did not fit their core focus of entertainment and acquired others that did. Their stock went up significantly.

These strategies are often viewed as add-ons in mature businesses when there is favoritism towards continuing with status quo business models. New business models have an inherent degree of risk and can be counter to the thinking of those who are comfortable with things as they always were.

Status quo business models (when they are working) should be retained but subject to *Continuous Improvements* (prototyping and validation), to ensure they do not become stagnant and that they represent a bridge for *Continuity* on the longer-term path to *resiliency* and *durability*.

It all comes down to five needs of the business (large and small) to be *durable:*

- Focus on customer requirements and the market.
- Calculation of accretive financial predictability.
- Access to innovative know-how teams (skill sets) and operational resources.
- Adoption of technological capabilities.
- Solidification of brand reputation.

I have always liked the following quote. It captures the essence of this chapter:

"The best way to predict your future is to create it" —Abraham Lincoln

I absolutely agree with Mr. Lincoln. Finding the way to accomplish this is the theme behind *The Quest for Durability / The Business Puzzle Method*™ approach. Change is difficult to accept, but it is doable.

My version:

Perpetual Planning and Continuous Improvement actions are the architects of your business's destiny.

For a business to have a *Durable Competitive Advantage*, it needs to focus on continuous transitional strategy development and timely tactical execution to adapt, change where it is necessary and grow.

A durable business is one that has substantiated plans for ongoing strategic direction that can be executed on your business's terms and within your business's timetable.

This describes leadership requirements of the future. Leaders will need to emphasize lifecycle durability (as a strategic imperative) as part of every business's growth strategy. Successful leaders (in all parts of a business) need to be visionaries with what was previously described in this book as having a *Durability Focused Mindset (DFM).*

Capturing great ideas from organizational functions needs to be considered in the context of the businesses culture. Ideas can percolate via teams or from individuals. How this happens is an assessment capability that is part of great leadership skills.

I recall an example while I was working in a Joint Venture in China. The HR department placed a Suggestion Box in the work area. None of the Chinese workers participated. No suggestions were received. That is not the way it is done in China. Ideas are surfaced via the team leader or not at all. Cultural sensitivity should always be a consideration when searching for a *Durability Focused Mindset (DFM).*

The Business Puzzle Method™ approach incorporates a framework that addresses the key elements needed to connect durability with transformational business strategy, covering formulation through execution. Successful leadership priorities need to be reflected in mission purpose, value statements, strategy emphasis and goals. I anticipate future changes in operating and business models to reflect social and environmental (in addition to standard messages normally published) as part of businesses internal and external communication plans (clearly articulated and collectively embraced). Durability transition strategies need to be linked with operational business strategies and workforce engagements of all kinds.

Long-term competitiveness requires aligning leadership priorities, strategies and tactical actions based on relevant insight, understanding, foresight and capabilities...the ongoing task of all workforce leadership.

A first-class strategic planning process such as *The Business Puzzle Method*™ approach will serve to focus a business on current *Relevant* and *Viable* vision, mission and goals. These can change to be expanded in scope or to reflect changes in direction. In any case, the ultimate universal leadership team goals in summary are *survival, growth, and satisfaction of customer, management and other stakeholder expectations* (including profitability).

The following are some of the most important *Durable Business Development* success outcomes that are transportable into the future:

- Maintaining a sustainable year-over-year Competitive Advantage.
- Establishing market share dominance.
- Delivering timely competitive *Customer Value Propositions.*
- Balancing *Continuity* (e.g. core business) activities with growth oriented programs.
- Justifying and sourcing funding requirements.
- Generating targeted operational performance and financial results.

- Building real-time insight, foresight, understanding and innovation into your business strategic planning and decision-making process.

- Customization of brand messages and actions to perpetuate customer confidence and trust needed to generate brand loyalty.

I am sure these outcomes are high priorities on your targeted accomplishments list! The reality is, they don't happen without an actionable synergistic *Perpetual Planning* methodology to make them happen.

Business success begins with leadership vision, substantiated via a well-crafted plan and implemented via actionable programs of execution.

Planned resiliency needs to be part of a business's vision and planning process.

Planned resiliency implies having Perpetual Rationale for year-over-year lifecycle durability

It should also produce a powerful credible argument for *Risk Mitigation* and to be *Performance Predictable (e.g. implies an ability to project outcomes in the future)*. In addition, *Planned Resiliency* is a practice that can be followed in disaster recovery and business resumption scenarios. It requires multiyear planning, frequently modified operational practices and a mindset for innovative decision-making, protecting the long-term value of a business's brand.

To be effective, Resiliency Planning (e.g. includes vision, mission, content and implementation) must cross over multiple functions and follow a clear, justifiable way of doing things. A Resilient business is best managed in an empowered *Agile culture* of cooperative planning and shared decision-making.

Note: Let's consider an *Agile culture* as one that evolves past entrenched thinking and status quo ways of doing things. It reflects a leadership and workforce style that drives expedited business transformation.

Resiliency is a key ingredient to developing timely, flexible *Business Models* and supportive products and services needed to be a growing sustainable business.

By following the principles in *The Business Puzzle Method*™ approach, it will be possible to develop and maintain a roadmap for sustainable outcomes supporting a perpetual *Competitive Edge. The Business Puzzle Method*™ approach is a problem solving, enabling Business Development approach to design and implement on-going ways to be successful in the marketplace in the long run.

Essential elements

Following the principles of *The Business Puzzle Method*™ approach will put your Strategies and Tactics out in plain sight for your organization and marketplace to understand and embrace. *The Business Puzzle Method*™ approach is a method and a framework to deliver a dynamic roadmap to achieve lifecycle *Durability*. The key to long-term success is understanding the customer and industry nuances needed to deliver customer solutions and improve your market presence and *Competitive Advantage. To do this you need to be* able to engage audiences according to what is relevant to them.

Your business idea can be an excellent idea, but unless it is developed and presented as a fully integrated program of growth following evolutionary cutting-edge paths to success (strategies, tactics and business models), it will not achieve and maintain a foothold in the marketplace.

The Business Puzzle Method™ approach includes a methodology for a planning process design born out of my years of serving in many aspects of *Business Development*. It follows interactive principles to present a position that is credible and compelling as needed to lay out the justification for winning strategic business direction. *The Business Puzzle Method*™ approach is based on a baseline of essential elements needed to be a growth enabling business, as follows:

The essential elements of great planning activities to be ready for the future:

- **Perpetual Planning:** to maintain prioritized, synergistic, growth-oriented strategies and tactics…following an ongoing transformation process as needed to pursue seamless short-term and longer-term growth and durability.

- **Continuous Improvement of Core Capabilities:** to modify, enhance, refine or redirect core legacy Business Models and products/service offerings when needed to be competitive.

- **Master Planning of Business Models and Products / Services:** to develop *Business Model Migration* strategic and tactical solutions and corresponding *Contingency Programs* to manage lifecycle longevity and evolving customer value propositions.

- **Always-Ready To Change:** to Redirect (pivot) and reset business strategic and tactical direction to be a relevant, resilient and durable customer destination.

- **Real-Time Prospecting:** to constantly increase knowledge, insight, understanding and foresight needed to respond to current and future customer development opportunities.

- **Agile Management, Governance and Decision-Making:** to operate in a culture of cross-functional innovation and *actionable (timely, flexible, relevant) ingenuity.*

- **Frequent and Continuous Communication:** to practice sharing data and information to increase awareness of vision, mission and goal comprehension and compliance… communication needs to be between internal and external ecosystem participants.

- **Milestone Planning, Tracking & Trajectory Measurement:** to showcase accomplishments, plans, and expectations.

- **On-going Contingency Planning and Risk-Mitigation Management:** to increase confidence in response to concerns of ambiguity, change, challenges, interruptions while addressing opportunities.

- **Due Diligence Readiness Documentation:** to be able to initiate or respond to information inquiries of all types in a timely manner.

- **Evidence-Based Substantiation:** to collectively justify rationale needed to gain support for strategies, tactics, valuation justification and funding needs.

By following these essential elements, your business will be more likely to be viewed as being "fundable" with increased creditworthiness …to include generating positive cash flow, rationalizing predictable profitable outcomes and showcasing industry leading performance measures—all of which are important requirements to be relevant, resilient and durable. Following *The Business Puzzle Method*™ approach framework will demystify the path to achieving year-over-year durable profitable growth which is critically important to maintaining a Competitive Advantage.

* * *

Future-Oriented Perpetual Planning and Continuous Improvement as Business Development Imperatives

Planning to be durable should always be an activity under construction.

So often change, challenges and opportunities appear to an unprepared business leadership team as something that just happened without warning. Nothing could be farther from the truth. Change is always happening, and opportunities are endless. Focused planning (in constant motion) will keep your business ahead of your industry's landscape developments. Stagnation and business failures are generally due to inflexible business plans and inadequate business models. These are problems that can't be corrected overnight, leaving businesses unprepared to respond when they occur.

Being able to respond to change and / or create a disruptive marketplace impact should be an imperative on every business's agenda...what I call a ***future-oriented*** **(FO)** approach. You should consider this a *Business Development Imperative* to achieve and maintain a substantial *competitive advantage.*

Generally speaking, your business's planning activities need to synergistically reinforce ongoing ***Transformational Business Models (TBM)*** appropriate for your specific business and industry. This requires an innovative cultural mindset, a workforce aligned on a common business purpose, and a view for the future to make it happen. **Durability** requires an ability to:

- Continually adapt to changes to survive challenges and interruptions while addressing opportunities.

- Build structure and alignment of purpose and innovative creativity.

- Validated strategic direction including realistic tactical execution.

- Ability to maximize strengths and continually look for new capabilities.

- Maintain a balance between short-term outcomes and longer-term goals.

- Lay a relevant and resilient foundation for year-over-year durable growth.

- Constantly questioning the lifecycle status quo strategies and business models.

- Build substantiated rationale to persuade others to accept plans.

Successful ***durable*** business development conclusions move at the pace that visionaries see change and identify new opportunities. In my experience, rapidly growing businesses become a dominant marketplace force by following methodically orchestrated strategic planning and follow-up tactical execution programs such as included in the framework of *The Business Puzzle Method*™ approach. It is a methodology designed for visionaries.

Durable business development plans survive reality when they are actionable, flexible, insightful, timely and justifiable.

When I was the Executive Director (now retired) of the iconic Enterprise Development Center (EDC) at New Jersey Institute of Technology

(NJIT), I could gauge how a business was progressing by the progress they were making in evolving their business plan. The EDC had more than 90 client companies (resident and nonresident) per year, a real good sample.

Companies were required to submit a business plan when they entered the EDC; therefore, it was easy for me and the EDC staff to periodically evaluate their progress. Those companies run by visionaries would generally have new strategic options being considered within a six-month time period and beyond. Some companies had completely changed their industry focus. The EDC was clearly a catalyst to encourage visionary thinking, an environment perfect for visionary leaders.

Whether you are building a startup, introducing a new business model, rejuvenating an existing product /service offering, you should test the idea before building your detailed business plan. Your ideas need to be flexible and open to change... subject to modifications...as your insight and understanding becomes clearer.

From my M&A due diligence days, I developed a preliminary evaluation questionnaire to test the extent of viability of a business's development strategies and tactics.

Business Model and Product / Service Necessary Ingredients:

- To Be: a customer need, desire and want solution.
- To Be: consistent with short-term and longer-term strategies.
- To Be: clear (all stakeholders) about short-term and longer-term goals.
- To Be: able to demonstrate milestones and dependencies for profitable growth.

- To Be: able to understand marketplace characteristics, competition and trends.

- To Be: able to verify plans to be a high-quality, cost-effective manufactured/sourced product/service solution.

- To Be: knowledgeable about leadership and staffing needs for all stages of lifecycle growth.

- To Be: a business with technical capabilities for near-term and longer-term operational requirements.

- To Be: able to offer products and services sold and serviced via anticipated channels and supply-chains.

- To Be: knowledgeable regarding source, use and extent of capital required for envisioned fund raising.

These information points will help determine and justify whether a business has a plausible business plan with a realistic business model (s). They represent content needed to complete strategic prioritization and as assumption input to *Durability Fit (DF)* analysis, the assessment of risk and the justification of business valuation. Most of all, *The Business Model Product / Service Necessary Ingredients* represent the foundation of information, understanding and insight needed for the preparation of necessary *Evidence-Based Substantiation (EDS)* so important for durability validation.

Strategies and tactical concepts should be tested and validated before major commitments in dollars and other resources are made. I call this activity as **Evidence and Validation Determination (EVD)** as a way to ascertain feasibility of business models and verifying all resources needed for execution requirements. **EVD** should test assumptions to verify customer / marketplace and business model fit vs:

- Design parameters.

- Development process.
- Manufacture / source approaches.
- Marketing and distribution options.
- Servicing requirements.
- Financial requirements.

It is best to conduct this activity before lengthy business plans are written. This approach will increase your business's confidence in the transition strategy being considered, assist in planning for resource timing requirements in addition to saving money.

Chapter 5: Eye on Growth and Value Creation
(Understanding Where To Go Next)

The hardest recurring task of high growth rate businesses is the design and operation of transition strategies and tactics of execution to stimulate GROWTH as measured by such things as market share, profitability and value appreciation.

Growth Sizing Considerations (GSC)

I previously discussed what I called a need for *Continual Future Needs Alignment (CFNA) to be Performance Predictable and Durable.* Growth sizing is an integral part of this.

Further on, I will be discussing THE FOUR FUNDAMENTAL LEVELS OF PREPARATION, phase #2 The proof-of-concept verification phase.

It should be emphasized that *Lifecycle Durability* is maintained by continually growing your business to meet current and future customer and marketplace demands. This is accomplished by first understanding the size of a business opportunity as it pertains to your business purpose, vision, mission and goals. Some screening insights needed to define *Growth Sizing Considerations (GSC)* include:

- Size and growth rate of the total industry.
- Extent of customers in target markets.
- Buying preferences of customers in target markets.

- Market position of embedded competitors.
- Sufficiency of resources to impact the marketplace.

This type of information forms the foundation for development of GROWTH oriented transition strategies (goals and objectives) and tactics. Access to this type of information will enhance your business's capability to make accurate forecast sales and make plans for resource requirements.

The need for synergistic business development to be compelling

Business success in today's world (and in your world going-forward) will require going beyond just producing financial performance metrics to be viewed as a successful business in the eyes of the many audiences.

In addition, rationale must go beyond just introducing customer product and service solutions...you will need partnerships, alliances, R&D collaborations, customer prepared channel arrangements, human capital recruiting, growth programs, and shareholder value substantiation to be compelling.

Your business's financial position and forecasts will need additional complementary justification for your *business plan (and supporting plans)* to be a marketplace and growth oriented decision-making baseline document. Strategies covering operational drivers (e.g. marketing, manufacturing / sourcing, supply chains, and development programs) need to be complementary to the overall strategic and tactical plans... quantifiable and displayed via the financial statements (and financial performance indicators) plus non-financial operational Key Performance Indicators (KPIs) appropriate for your industry.

THE NEED FOR AN EXPEDITED CHANGE PROCESS

In today's world and the world of the future, change, competitive pressures and demographic preferences are occurring at an increasingly fast pace. This requires business models and product /service customer solutions delivered via what I call *Expedited Innovation Practices (EIP)*. As an industry grows, there is a tendency for the marketplace leaders to become complacent...again look at Sears, Blockbuster and Kodak. For the observant business, this scenario invites new opportunity.

Expedited Innovation Practices (EIP) lead to continuous commercialization (new and new and improved business models, products, services and strategic actions) practices to be in what I call a *Perpetual Reset Mode (PRM)* to address frequent planned and unplanned change, challenges and opportunities. This is a practice followed by businesses in the mobile cellphone marketplace. It is an effective business model to follow.

Lifecycle Durable businesses should always have some portion of their business in a STARTUP MODE.

FINANCING ALTERNATIVES FOR BUSINESS EXPANSION

Business Development plans need to be justifiably and synergistically linked to financial sourcing options to be considered a lifecycle durable business.

Durability is best achieved by combining ***organic growth*** business strategies (growth utilizing ***Continuous Improvement*** of existing business models and capabilities) and ***inorganic growth*** which relies on focused ***Perpetual Planning*** practice outcomes for growth by following strategies external to your business (e.g. M&A, Joint Ventures, opening new territories, introducing new types of business models).

Building the right mix of ***organic*** and ***inorganic*** growth plans is a mission-critical strategic challenge that needs to be part of all business's planning-processes...before stagnation or shortfalls of performance outcomes in addressable markets becomes a reality. Logically organized business development planning synergies will be required.

Business growth and marketplace survival requires following ***Perpetual Planning*** practices combined with ***Continuous Improvement*** of core capabilities *to be* ***Always-Ready*** and ***Performance Predictable*** *as needed to change strategic direction (pivoting) in a timely manner.*

An argument to grow.

THE BIG PICTURE

Entrepreneurial business innovation is an enabler centered on creating / retaining jobs, building communities, creating health enhancing breakthroughs and growing the economy. Yes, this is a big picture view of why business development (for businesses of all sizes) is high on my priority list. Contributing to economic growth is an endeavor with a true purpose. Going forward, these are reasons of equal or greater concern to customer and investor stakeholder communities alike.

THE INDIVIDUAL BUSINESS SOLUTION

Business growth is an indicator of the degree of acceptance of business models in the marketplace.

One of the first things I learned from my experience in the investor community is the importance of year-over-year GROWTH! Year-over-year business growth (not just sporadic growth spirits) is vital to achieving lifecycle durability. *Business Growth* is an indicator of the capability to produce future *durable* performance…it's an indicator to substantiate your business's ability to:

- Prove credibility of strategies and tactics.
- Validate marketplace receptiveness of business models.

- Substantiate market share success.
- Demonstrate ability to outperform competitors.
- Add rationale to justify valuation.

Business Growth highlights what your business is good at.

A Growth business generally has the ability to stimulate customer repeat business and customer retention, two strong indicators of resiliency and durability.

Business Growth is a predictor of the health of a business

Business Growth happens because of the ability to attract continuous high-quality sources of revenue, net of customer attrition (called revenue churn). Total Business Growth requires top-line revenue growth, increased margins and the generation of cash and bottom-of-the line profitability. For this reason, *Business Growth* is one of the first things to review when taking a more granular look at the extent of business viability. Understanding revenue churn as it pertains to Business Growth is a key indicator of resiliency and durability.

Following *The Quest for Durability / The Business Puzzle Method*™ approach will help your business develop a systematic method to instill disciplines, practices and principles needed to deliver growth and lifecycle durability.

Stimulating high growth is accomplished by differentiating your business to reflect the realities of the day and of the future.

A WORD ABOUT FLEXIBILITY and PIVOTING

To keep pace with these growth requirements, a methodology and a discipline is necessary at the grass-roots level (e.g. individual businesses, corporations and organizations). Durability requires continual actions to be insightful, knowledgeable and confident to change direction as required or as planned.

Your ability to extend your *Business's Lifecycle Longevity* into the future requires an ability to pursue new opportunities even when confronted with marketplace and industry changes, challenges and interruptions.

The greatest challenge your business has is growing to survive into the future. Year-over-year ***GROWTH*** *is the key indicator of strategic viability needed for survival…based on compelling, realistic and defendable justification.*

To ensure future viability, you need to follow the principles of *Perpetual Planning* and *Continuous Improvement* of operations and marketplace practices, as emphasized in *The Business Puzzle Method*™ approach…*a way to find and maintain a path to Durability.* This will keep your strategic and tactical planning focus on those items that are important to understand and pursue those things that define the best *Blueprint* to maintain a *relevant*, *resilient* and *durable Competitive Edge.*

As a starting point, create multiple recurring revenue streams as a way to deflect such things as unplanned competition, economic slowdowns or other forms of business interruptions. In addition, it is important to be *Always-Ready* to counteract marketplace competitive trends leading to a *Commoditized Business Model* (e.g. loss of unique identity and easily substituted by customers) which will significantly slow growth—or worse yet, result in a downward spiral.

Perhaps most important, don't get preoccupied with maintaining legacy *Business Model* status quo, especially if the marketplace is trending towards commoditization (e.g. loss of unique identity, pricing / margin advantage and your competitive edge).

Take advantage of such things as growing the number of channels available to marketers and sales teams, thus improving your ability to continually *prospect* for insight, understanding and tactical validation. In addition, fill your *innovation pipeline* with cross-functional input by following an *Agile collaborative decision-making process* where applicable.

Unlocking the *Resilient* potential of your business is the secret to *Future-Proofing* your business, which includes finding new ways to attract additional revenue.

You will not know the potential of your business unless you follow a *Strategic Plan Formulation* program that is *Agile*, innovative and customer and industry specific. *The Business Puzzle Method*™ approach is such a program.

The longer-term view.

If your business is not growing but staying within the parameters of your original core business definition, your business is vulnerable to change, challenges and interruptions!

Longer-term Business Models have the characteristic of being able to compete on capabilities, features and function, differentiation and cost. When properly positioned in your *Customer Engagement Process (CEP)*, typically makes them a desired customer solution and a marketplace success. If not, you should consider removing, replacing or modifying your core *Business Model* comfort zone as needed to be positioned for growth. By following this *Continuous Improvement Business Development Practice* (CIBDP), you will be able to focus your business on faster growing, more profitable customer solutions. This requires continuous expansion of innovative capabilities to fit strategic transformation opportunities...developed from within innovative organizations with creative cultures...a prerequisite for a lifecycle durable long-term competitive advantage.

Some of my recommended methods to extend your core *Business Model* definition are as follows:

FOOD FOR THOUGHT – PREPARE A CUSTOMIZED BUSINESS GROWTH PLAN

Substantiated plans demonstrating growth momentum add confidence in a business for such things as making shareholders happy, attracting and retaining employees, encouraging customer loyalty and addressing strategic opportunities.

Consider BUSINESS GROWTH as a "Proof of Concept" to make your business be viewed as FUNDABLE (meets requirements of funding sources) and strategically successful.

A *Business Growth Plan* emphasizes your path to growth and your business's "Sweet Spot"...the rationale to achieve and maintain a lasting *competitive advantage.*

Business Growth is the critical ingredient to justify lifecycle durability.

Ways to define growth strategies are numerous. A sampling is as follows:

- Add/revise business models.
- Expand territory of operation.
- Add sales from additional customer segments.
- Offer differentiated products and services.
- Find value-added strategic partners and alliances.
- Utilize social media customer contact capabilities.
- Modify brand messages.
- Rebranding.

- Create a customer loyalty program.
- Implement a referral program.
- Create a franchising program.
- Enhance sales lead generation capabilities.
- Business combinations (mergers, acquisitions and takeovers).

How strategies such as these would work in your industry for your business should be a topic of your *Perpetual Planning* decision-making process. Start by researching your industry leaders and competitors and build a prioritized disruptive GROWTH PLAN (incorporating the learnings determined from following *The Business Puzzle Method*™ approach) of your own business strategies and tactics. Determine opportunities and move to address them. Be creative and dream, fast-growing successful businesses typically follow a combination of growth strategies similar to those listed previously.

* * *

A Growth Plan is a plan of action and serves as evidence of forward-looking insight and understanding,

When I evaluate a business, I always look for growth plans as evidence that the business understands the industry and the logic driving their strategic direction leading to lifecycle longevity and year-over-year durability.

Lifecycle Durability means focusing on how your business can deliver disruptive market entries with lifecycle longevity characteristics.

Business Growth – Always a Work in Progress

Your business's demonstrated ability to successfully grow through ALL lifecycle phases is a critical requirement to be considered a durable business entity.

The Durable Growth Plan

Growth Plans (combined with) tactical execution actions are vital to your business's *durability*. Properly prepared *Growth Plans* can strengthen business capabilities and can move a business from stagnation (or potential stagnation) caused by over reliance on status quo / legacy business positions to ones that reinforce and expand *Market Share* and *Competitive Advantage*.

Durable growth means continually creating value for your business and in the marketplace for your customers.

Consider these initial questions:

- Which growth plan would be the most favorable for your business?
- How does it fit with the current & future business strategies, tactics and historical performance?
- What are the timelines for implementation and operation?
- What is the extent of funding requirements, resources and returns anticipated (financial and operational)?

As I stated previously, when I perform a business assessment, I like to see a *growth plan* (strategic and tactical) as a specific addendum to a business's overall b*usiness plan*.

Growth plans need focused attention…separate from day-to-day operational plans and actions. The presentation of a *Growth Plan* satisfies a primary due diligence check confirming recognition that the business leaders understand the future needs of their business / industry and are preparing to address the same.

The Financial Reality of Growth

Lifecycle Growth constantly requires capital funding which can be derived from multiple sources. Plans without adequate funding source (s) will not succeed in reaching their goals! In addition, funding source types will vary depending on business model lifecycle stages of growth. Consider a partial money sourcing menu of possibilities:

- *Banks & lines-of-credit*
- *Grants*
- *Investors*
- *Venture capitalists*
- *Shareholders*

Business *Plans* need to be developed in conjunction with plans to source funding requirements. One of the points of true genius in growing a business is being able to produce and/or obtain adequate funding in the appropriate timeframes. This can be done in a variety of ways. However, in all cases, your business will need a VALIDATED BUSINESS PLAN to substantiate your businesses funding request. Following the *Quest for Durability / The Business Puzzle Method*™ approach will give your business a *Lifecycle Durability Proof of Concept...* information to substantiate your business strategy, tactical execution programs, funding amounts and timing of needs.

I have experienced CEOs who believe that business growth is the responsibility of the marketing department. Actually, it is a business development task of all functional organizations in the entire business as formulated via *The Business Puzzle Method*™ approach.

Substantiated business plans form the forecasting assumptions driving the logic to justify attracting interest needed for financial sourcing.

There are numerous ways to grow a business, some more complex and time consuming than others. All are best developed and evaluated by following *The Business Puzzle Method*™ principles of *Perpetual Planning* and *Continuous Improvement* of core capabilities. They can be categorized in two main areas, *Organic* and *Inorganic.*

Organic Growth Methods: Let's define organic growth as following internally (or externally) available resources and practices to improve performance—to achieve such things as revenue growth, margin improvements, better cash flow, and operational efficiencies.

You might call this obtaining *Funding from Existing Momentum*!

This can be done by changing such things as marketing plans (promotional programs), manufacturing / sourcing practices, packaging "look and feel," and pricing offerings.

Inorganic Growth Methods: Conversely, let's define inorganic growth as employing programs such as Mergers & Acquisition (M&A), Joint Ventures (JVs), alliances, and even opening new locations.

You might call this obtaining *Funding via Strategic Initiatives.*

The focus is having the capability to grow by such things as expanding into new markets, adding technical capabilities, acquiring new customers, expanding technical know-how and adding intellectual property. Implementation of *Inorganic* strategies generally requires a team of specialists (lawyers, bankers, and negotiators) not always part of a normal business organization unless *Inorganic* strategic growth programs are included as part of the *business development decision-making* process.

Hybrid Growth Plans

In my experience, the fastest growing businesses typically follow a combination of *Organic* and *Inorganic* growth strategies, as a way to be *resilient* and *durable.* These businesses have learned to simultaneously deal with short-term and long-term business improvements and growth challenges.

In all cases, a business should concentrate on continual business model rejuvenation and expansion by whatever means fits customer / marketplace evolution solutions... aligned according to specific business capabilities at a point in time. It is all about finding the best way (s) to improve efficiencies and address opportunities.

Growth Plans need to include financing considerations (source and use of funds) to be part of key strategic objectives and action plans...to achieving lifecycle durability goals.

Chapter 6 Barriers, Impediments & Stagnation

(Overcoming Resistance To Durability Success)

Dealing with Endless Business Problems and Pressure Points

As a Business Development professional (business owner, corporate executive, advisor), you often feel you are operating in a world of uncertainty.

Between dealing with technology advancements, new channels and supply-chain introductions, and evolving regulations, your day is full. In addition, leadership time demands can be challenged by employee issues, and especially from customer related matters. To deal with these situations, a business needs to employ a *Durability Mindset* to be prepared with *Business Model Migration* and *Contingency Plan* strategies. In addition, when you enhance economic development, everyone benefits.

The Businesses Failure Trap

The number one reason I hear for a business's poor performance, stagnation, slow business growth or business failure is I RAN OUT OF CASH!!!

This is typically true. However, very seldom are the *Root-Cause* reasons for running out of cash ever openly discussed. The lack of cash (working capital) is a resultant situation driven by a variety of marketplace and/or operational reasons leading to stagnation and business failure.

Durability requires shifting business models, product / service offerings and essential operational practices as frequently as necessary to gain and protect marketplace traction and an overall long-term competitive advantage.

By following the principles of *The Business Puzzle Method*™ approach your business can avoid the business failure trap. *Perpetual Planning* and *Continuous Improvement* practices encourage constant vigilance needed to determine which strategies and tactics will create the most business value (considering the degree of risk) within the constraints of a business's available and obtainable resources and capabilities.

Shifting, expanding and adding business models… with the purpose of maximizing value propositions…should be a way of life for a business on a growth trajectory. In addition, your business will be more confident in estimating revenue, costs, expenses and investments.

Understanding Root-Cause reasons for business stagnation / failures in your industry (and subsequently addressing them) is a strategy imperative for business success.

Root-Cause reasons behind business stagnation / failure seen most often:

Every business in every industry has warning signs (root-cause reasons) of pending performance problems that need to be watched and managed as part of the planning process.

Following *The Business Puzzle Method*™ approach will allow your business to plan for and make the best use of assets, resources and capabilities in a timely manner. Keeping tabs on Root-Cause reasons for failure (and correcting the same in real time) needs to be a part of your business's decision-making process.

Most of the time, it is not the lack of availability of funding that causes a business to fail, but instead it is the lack of shortcomings in strategic and tactical plans making confidence in achievement of operational goals and maintaining projected profitability performance outcomes of concern.

As a starting point, have a look at the following list of Root-Cause reasons some business fail:

- Customer / buyer / user vs business fit not compatible.
- Business Model (s) not validated or kept current.
- Lack of short-term to longer-term strategic continuity.
- Limited planning for growth funding needs.
- Incompatible culture resisting change.
- Missed key milestones.
- Lack of a customer development & retention process.
- Gaps in know-how staffing and other resource requirement needs.
- Risk mitigation plans not prepared.
- Poor preparation for growth opportunity due diligence discussions.
- Business model (s) & transition initiatives not compelling or durable.
- Valuation, strategy & executional tactical rationale not justifiable.

This list was extracted from my notes over the years and as the Executive Director of the EDC at NJIT for more than a decade, I had extensive exposure to this topic. These items were often part of discussions with line-of-credit sources. When missed, more collateral was required.

In addition, when I was in the M&A business, I used these shortcomings as weaknesses allowing for discounting of valuation and consideration during negotiation discussions.

For these reasons, I included them as major points of emphasis in *The Business Puzzle Method*™ approach. The extent that they have been addressed will increase a business's viability and degree of quality perception.

Root-Cause failure preventative measures can be dealt with by following the *Business Puzzle Method*™ approach. This approach will allow for identification of Root-Cause potential failure gaps, prioritize and the taking of corrective actions leading to lifecycle longevity and durability and a justifiable competitive advantage.

The inherent practices within *The Business Puzzle Method*™ approach will allow for estimating and planning for the source, use and timing of cash requirements. Both on-going and growth *Business Model* programs require levels of cash. All programs have conflicting impacts on budgeting and financing requirements. By following the principles of planning included in *The Business Puzzle Method*™ approach, resources and monetary requirements can be planned, justified, and prioritized.

The Reluctance to Encourage Advanced Planning Discussions

So often strategic planning discussions that produced potential strategic plans were filed in binders but never consistently implemented.

The fact is that in order to survive and be a market leader, you need to continually be ready to reframe and /or expand your business as needed to adapt.

Not following this principle represents a serious breakdown in the *Business Development* process. Missed opportunities, resources not available when needed and loss of market share and a *Competitive Edge* is typically what happens when needed strategic and tactical plans are ignored.

By following the principles of *The Business Puzzle Method*™ approach there will be ample data/information available to determine the best courses of action. I recommend following a practice of determining the *net contribution* to the business of *Strategic* and *Tactical* plans, prior to implementation.

I include a review process in *The Business Puzzle Method*™ approach practices which I call *Feasibility Validation Studies* (FVS). These are tradeoff reviews of scenario evaluations. Results are a necessary input to a business's *decision-making* activities. Adhering to this process will help determine validation of assumptions, projected financial requirements, overall performance forecasts plus the degrees of *Risk Mitigation* possible.

Critical *Milestone* progress should be analytically validated based on milestone results and conclusions ascertained from *Feasibility Validation Studies (FVS)*. *Business Model Lifecycle Longevity* (period from launch through expansion to eventually being obsolete) is best managed by applying frequent validation study reviews vs *Milestone* progress. In fact, the longevity of a *business in total* is dependent on the sustainability of current and future *Business Models*.

The Removal of Internal Barriers to Growth and Durability

Durable growth requires continual innovative transition to reach and maintain long-term visions.

Lifecycle Durability happens when you focus your business strategies and tactics of execution on current and future customer satisfaction. This requires innovation and actionable follow-through.

Rapidly expanding businesses drive change with innovative business models, not just react to landscape changes and competitive pressures. Each industry has its own multidimensional influences and barriers. The following are some common themes to consider.

It has been my experience that high-performing businesses have distinctive defining governance traits leading to:

- Timely, flexible, speedy decision-making capabilities.
- Collaborative functional organization structure.
- Culture of innovation creating new and/or improved Business Models.
- Focus on continuous value creation (overall business and customer solutions).

The *Quest for Durability / The Business Puzzle Method*™ approach (as a durability enabler) will serve to break down barriers in a synergistic way.

Perpetual Planning and Continuous Improvement Strategies to Remove Barriers

Points of Emphasis

Deliver needed customer solutions

Only business models that are customer-facing will have the flexibility to meet requirements to deliver timely customer preferred solutions. In this fast-moving landscape, perpetual prospecting (real-time market research) is required to remain relevant, resilient and durable.

Maximize revenue

Revenue (recurring and nonrecurring) can be increased in multiple ways. Strategic and tactical formation plans need to focus on options for both revenue growth and for defensive reasons…to combat competitive price

pressures or other competitive strategies. Apple always has new products, functions and features available to stay ahead of the competitive curve. It is one of their competitive advantages.
Establish & maintain targeted marketplace leadership and grow market / segment share.

Growth programs should always be part of *Perpetual Planning* and *Continuous Improvement* of core capabilities activities (in addition to day-to-day activities) to enhance your business's *competitive advantage.* They can take many forms such as organic strategies which typically encompasses modifications to maximize existing business models... adding new products, changing customer service approaches, developing alternate advertising & promotion programs or implementing inorganic strategies...mergers & acquisitions, expanding into new locations / territories, joint ventures. Close insight, understanding and know-how capabilities and knowledge gaps.

Adding knowledgeable human capital resources, and technological capabilities to increase marketplace intelligence and understanding, will always be an ongoing requirement to keep up with the fast moving, changing landscape. Transformational leadership (in all functions of your business) will be the drivers of *durability*. Communicate frequently to unlock pent-up innovation and personal innovation and communication actions.

Enhance efficiency and control cost

Improving efficiency should be part of your *Continuous Improvement* initiatives agenda. It should include actions such as improving margins, simplifying workflow, enhancing the customer engagement process, manufacturing or sourcing practices or just maximizing the use of your business's tangible and intangible resources.

Cost reductions should eliminate nonessential things that do not match the needs of strategic and tactical plans. Before eliminating, always consider repurposing as a way to utilize resources or substituting resources between products / services or between business entities.

Create and maintain required cash-flow and profitability

Cash-flow demands (inflows and outflows) represent real numbers and are critical influencers driving short-term and longer-term strategy formulation prioritization. Strategy formulation has to consider such things as product / services sales, pricing, customer payment forecasts, inventory practices, and vendor agreement terms and conditions. Positive cash-flow means you can operate and grow your business. Negative cash-flow signals a red-flag.

Like any potential lender or investor, I look at cash-flows (especially growth rate of cash flows) as an indicator of a business's ability to maintain current levels of operations, secure financing, attract investors, and potentially be able to grow. I consider cash-flow statements as the key document from financial analysis, especially the "cash burn rate" projections (rate cash is being utilized).

Profitability (an accounting term) on the other hand, is not as valuable a performance indicator, but still required by most business evaluators. Profitability (sometimes called paper profits) includes non-cash transactions (depreciation and amortization) which lowers tax liabilities. Depreciation is not something you can spend. Profitability calculations also can include accruals and entries anticipated in the future.

In some circumstances profitability can be considered more important. Consider a publicly traded business where share price is pegged to profits and growth of profits. Details of these ramifications is beyond the intent of this book but does influence *durability*.

Be prepared for change, challenges, interruptions and opportunities

All business models have a limited **lifecycle longevity**. Marketplace changes, disruptive products and services, evolving customer preferences impact the ability of all businesses to retain market share and a durable *Competitive Advantage*. Only through **continuous prospecting** (real-time market research) can a business stay informed and ultimately maintain **year-over-year durability.**

The best practice is to be aware of marketplace developments and business opportunities before your competitors become aware...then execute your most appropriate version of business model differentiation. **Business Models** need to be *relevant*, *flexible*, and *timely*. The marketplace is not a constant.

In addition, your business in total also has a *Lifecycle Expectation* which should be given constant attention. *Business Lifecycles* around the world are getting shorter...in some industries faster than others. *Status quo* business models (unless modified) generally will not carry your business to a position of being a **long-term durable** entity. Your business needs clearly defined growth programs as a priority to be considered *durable.*

Demonstrate assurance and verification of strategies and tactics

By following a perpetual planning process, as is included in ***The Business Puzzle Method***™ approach, it will be possible to phase-in *"New and Improved"* ways of satisfying customer requirements along with dealing with day-to-day business activities. Business decision-making methodologies need to produce such things as business plans (operations, marketing, development, and manufacturing / sourcing) trial results, demonstration conclusions and feasibility studies to justify strategic direction options proposed. This approach will generate add-on value (for the total business and for customer solutions).

Durability requires the continual preparation of logic and rationale to increase positive business perceptions and present negotiation material to substantiate business valuation. I call this **Evidence-Based Substantiation (EBS).**

Minimize risks

All business plan reviewing parties have a level of risk tolerance. Preparation to deal with possible risk-averse reviewer conclusions can be minimized by preparing **Contingency Plans** and alternative strategic **Migration Plans**. This approach (when included in your business's decision-making process) will keep your business from committing business suicide due to incomplete planning practices. Your goal is to keep your business relevant in good times and bad times.

Presentations of Business Plan Strategies and Tactics need to emphasize the **Risk Mitigation** logic built into the strategic thinking driving **Business Model** direction. Of significant importance will be the understanding of the extent of seamless connections between *short-term* actions, goals and *longer-term continuity*.

Durable growth requires removing dysfunctional operational dynamics.

Often businesses place too much emphasis on short-term objectives that ultimately alienate customers. They are not considering the long-term effect of their actions. Case in point:

You may recall the earlier reference to an incident from my days in a corporate market management organization. I received a considerable number of complaints about one particular Call Center. According to the complaints, they were not solving their customer concerns. I went to visit the Call Center site to investigate the situation. I learned that the complaints occurred because of a Call Center measurement practice that required Call Center operators to terminate a customer call after a specific period of time, regardless of the status of the call resolution conversation.

This practice was explained to me by the Call Center management team as a labor-saving practice that could be measured in less staffing requirements and less overtime needed. Certainly, the Call Center management thought they had good intentions. This was a legacy business practice implemented as a cost reduction policy. Unfortunately, this practice ignored their real purpose which was customer satisfaction leading to customer loyalty and repeat business.

Chapter 7: Putting the Pieces Together

(The Principles Of *The Business Puzzle Method*™ Approach)

In summary, The Quest for Durability / The Business Puzzle Method™ ***approach is a fact-based, compelling methodology to build a persuasive blueprint for year-over-year, lifecycle durability.***

Critical thinking: A few years ago, I taught a course on ***"Critical Thinking"*** at a major international corporation. I remember emphasizing the importance of systematically collecting data/information from multiple sources, sharing perspectives in a decision-making process and communicating strategy and tactics within a culture focused on relevancy and solving problems. I personally retained this perspective throughout my business career and have adopted the concepts of ***"Critical Thinking"*** as a foundation principle in *The Business Puzzle Method*™ approach. It is part of my *DNA*.

Note: In this application, Critical Thinking is being used as a form of problem-solving by collecting information / data, analyzing information / data and drawing conclusions about courses of action.

This best practice thinking supports a main theme of *The Business Puzzle Method*™ approach (e.g. *Perpetual Planning* and core capabilities *Continuous Improvement)* as needed to produce *evidence-based* plans required to substantiate and reinforce relevant, resilient, durable strategies and tactics.

By following *The Business Puzzle Method*™ approach you will be preparing what I call a ***Blueprint for Strategic and Tactical Success (BSTS).*** This is a foundation principle of *The Business Puzzle Method*™

approach and an important component of the *"Show Me"* aspect for those desiring to use the output of *The Business Puzzle Method*™ approach as a *Persuasion Tool*...to develop and defend strategic and tactical justification while increasing credibility. It will prove useful when seeking corporate budget approvals or growth capital.

Not too long ago I was watching a crew install a prefabricated house, which in the industry is called a prefab. Their *Business Model* included a full marketing promotion program, customer satisfaction design process and offsite construction product source, thus producing a detailed *Blueprint* for tactical execution and *cross-functional work plans (e.g. designers, carpenters, roofers, crane operators, truck drivers)*. By working from a *Blueprint with a clear purpose and goals, synergistic resource utilization, customer verified directional solutions*, this company consistently delivers high quality customer satisfaction...with an excellent book of referral business, leading to being a *durable* competitive business. Building a *Blueprint* with a well communicated (internal and external to the business) work plan was their method for ensuring tactical success. Without this approach to customer satisfaction, they could not maintain their *Competitive Advantage*. A great example to follow.

If you agree that your business should strive to operate a year-over-year *relevant*, *resilient* and *durable* business, begin preparing a ***Blueprint for Strategic and Tactical Success (BSTS)*** of your own. Reaching and maintaining ongoing *Relevancy*, *Resiliency* and *Durability* is not a one-time event. A blueprint should be designed to meet the multiple needs of customers, employees, investors, partners, vendors and other stakeholders. The ***BSTS*** should be creative, BRIEF, fact-based and easily comprehensible. Have a look at my checklist from my M&A days as follows:

* * *

Key Ingredients: Blueprint for a Strategic and Tactical Success (BSTS) Document

- Business purpose, vision, mission and goals.
- Previous and forward-looking strategies and tactics (short-term and longer-term).
- Value proposition clarity.
- Key team members and role responsibilities.
- Customer and marketplace needs to be addressed.
- Major milestones and accomplishments to-date.
- Strategic and tactical information sources.
- Advertising and promotion campaigns.
- Marketing and sales approach.
- Product and service development, manufacturing and sourcing programs.
- Technology requirements.
- Financial plan and financial performance to-date.

I would also have available Due Diligence Assessment Readiness Materials (Puzzle Piece Principle # 11) that will be discussed in a later chapter of this book. Plus, include Business Plan and supporting operational plans (e.g. marketing, product development, staffing, manufacturing / sourcing, human resources) in an abbreviated form. In addition, assumptions driving the sales forecast will need to be explained. A "bottoms-up" forecast is always preferred.

As a thing to do right away, start to create your business's compelling ***Blueprint for Strategic and Tactical Success (BSTS)*** to cover your business's own prioritized strategic and tactical formulation plans... which will have considerable backup, justification, synergistic support components and substantiation resulting from following *The Business Puzzle Method*™ approach. Work on your business's ***BSTS*** needs to become a constant work in progress.

An Additional Definition

A *Blueprint for Strategic and Tactical Success (BSTS)* is unique for every business and industry. It is the product of insight and knowledge obtained from *Perpetual Planning* and *Continuous Improvement* activity. A *BSTS* outlines the execution pathway to reach short-term and longer-term goals. It specifies actions and tasks needed to implement the Business Plan and supporting linked plans (e.g. marketing, financial, human resources, and technologies). Business Plans are one thing but what is needed to implement the business plan is another. A *BSTS* is a great communication tool delineating actions, organizational handoffs and needs to be done (when, timelines, costs and by whom). A *BSTS* showcases tactical execution of previously discussed *Evidence-Based Transformation* strategies and plans...an actionable translation of business plans.

The Business Puzzle Method™

I would like to begin on a personal note. In my years of experience, I have noticed that there is no set formula for Business Development commercialization, course correction and business model statement updates—only multiple paths to follow which may or may not work in a given situation. Finding that path is the task of all venture company founders, CEOs and C-suite leaders. Financial investors and strategic investors will recognize the path that fits their expectations and fund and support a company accordingly. During my years as a corporate M&A transaction leader, business planning/financial executive, a business owner, business angel, executive director of one of the largest and most successful multi-development stage incubators / business development centers in the U.S.A., and co-founder and member of an angel network, I have seen a pattern of logical business requirements that when met will generate realistic ecosystem interest.

As an experienced member of the business development ecosystem over a long period of time, I have seen a pattern of "must haves" that should always be considered by any entrepreneur seeking to scale/grow a financially sustainable business. I will refer to these "must haves" as components of *The Business Puzzle Method*™ approach throughout this book. I have prepared explanations for ease in determining growth company business readiness, designed to increase chances of reaching goals in a fast-changing marketplace. This is a book for a diverse audience, applicable for tech and non-tech-based companies in seed, early stage, expansion and mature stages of growth. The principles portrayed in this book are applicable as a baseline for company initial strategic reviews and/or on-going updates to existing strategic plans.

When building and growing a business (subsidiary or business unit) regardless of how mature the business is, you need to include an Agile Management team with like-minded support organizations, all with complementary skills. These professionals need to be able to work as cross-organizational partners, to understand customer feedback data/information, combined with competitive and environmental scan knowledge, in addition to their basic professional skills. Developing an Agile organization is a major challenge for successful business leadership.

For an agile culture to develop, it is necessary to break down silos that cause roadblocks and produce resistance throughout a business. Companies favoring silo types of operations are the opposite of operations favoring open teamwork. In my experience, silos have a tendency to make functional organizations competitors of a sort, following a behavioral mindset that stifles creativity, causes frustrations and slows progress.

For this reason, a business favoring a culture of *teamwork* embracing a *Durability Focused Mindset (DFM)* as discussed previously, is the year-over-year durability approach to follow.

Team-building practices are not easy to initiate. However, they should be a high priority quality practice for a business following *Continuous Improvement* planning practices. It is one of my obsessions. Start by:

- Setting goals as a team.
- Implementing training programs.
- Setting up frequent and easy communication programs.
- Adopting a practice of sharing decision-making.

Following this approach will have a significant impact on the year-over-year durability of your business.

* * *

DESIGNING YOUR BUSINESS FOR LIFECYCLE DURABILITY

Lifecycle Durability is made possible by adding Agile business practices as a Continuous Improvement business practice.

For a business to achieve lifecycle durability success, a business needs to ***continuously reinvent itself*** *to future-proof its business and find ways to win in the marketplace (a Perpetual Planning philosophy).* This means having a playbook producing the ability to anticipate and address market developments (in a timely manner), align the business to create innovate breakthroughs while operating in a customer-focused collaborative culture. Yes, this sounds like *The Business Puzzle Method*™ approach.

The Business Puzzle Method™ approach can be enhanced by including ***Agile Team Skill Sets*** to the mix. In this context, I define Agile practices as a way to work together.

- Team alignment with shared vision.
- Cross-functional collaborative representation.
- Shared goals and accountability.
- Frequent shared communication.

I recommend employing *Agile practices* to areas of your business where rapid response is required. How *Agile practices* are best deployed is a decision unique to a specific business and industry. It is a methodology to produce *Continuous Improvement* as part of your business's *Perpetual Planning* decision-making process.

In my business travels around the world, I am always in the mode of continuous learning. One thing especially caught my attention was the impact of *Agile* business practices on job satisfaction and in business performance results. I therefore added the extent of *Agile* business practices observed to my evaluation criteria checklist.

Unless your business is a very small business, it is very hard to implement *Agile* practices in all parts of your business. It requires a culture of acceptance and a *Durability Focused Mindset (DFM)* to be workable. Business-wide adoption is an eventual goal but should not be the initial goal.

A business's lasting durability depends on the ability to stay on the cutting edge of what customers prefer, what society needs in addition to what stakeholders and funding sources demand.

Business Lifecycle Durability is increased by introducing Agile practices as another way to create a recurring Competitive Advantage...the ability to stimulate growth momentum, innovate quickly and shorten "Time to Market" plans.

Any degree of adoption of *Agile* practices should be part of a *Continuous Improvement* of core capabilities initiatives, such as is included in *The Business Puzzle Method*™ approach. *The Business Puzzle Method*™ addresses the utilization of Agile practices as a necessary component of culture adjustments, organization alignment and it is most effective in functional organizations that need to adapt to change, challenges and interruptions quickly...to form innovative strategies and business models. It sounds too logical to be ignored. However, whenever there is a need to change the way people do things, there will always be pushback and resistance.

The worst obstacle to business growth and success is in entrenched organizations that have historically been organized and operated in a silo hierarchy, making them risk prone. This is a cultural issue that needs to be organized and aligned to accommodate a different kind of work environment.

Ideas originate from everywhere. Encourage open communication and feedback.

Due to the rapid rate of changes in the marketplace, it will eventually be necessary to reinvent and modify a company's strategic thinking. The *Business Puzzle Method*™ is intended to be a "living" planning tool to assist in this endeavor. It is designed to be revisited and periodically updated. Companies in all stages of growth can reach unwanted roadblocks or are experiencing static growth. By continually working to understand the customer(s) and marketplace rules of the game, a company can eliminate obstacles and roadblocks. A company should always be searching for the most current relevant realities! Collective knowledge will dictate strategy. Business Model Statement evaluations and plan execution will be the key to successful outcomes.

Plan for and make strategic Business Model Statement changes, and plan execution program changes as needed, before competition requires your company to make changes in order for your company to survive.

In order to reduce the risk of investing in your company, a lender or investor will need to VALIDATE your company's plans and assumptions.

They can start with the ***Blueprint for Strategic and Tactical Success (BSTS)*** as previously discussed in an earlier chapter. This approach will increase substantiation and/or emphasize proven experience a business has as evidence of business durability.

Plans survive marketplace evolution and changing customer preferences when they are flexible, insightful, timely and justifiable.

THE REALITY OF DEALING WITH A CUSTOMER - DEFINED FUTURE

Continually work to validate and strengthen the puzzle pieces of *The Business Puzzle Method*™ approach, to include details such as customer needs, prices, services policies, technical solutions, and other sales/revenue and cost/expense model drivers. Knowledge, combined with risk mitigation analysis, will serve to be *Outcome Predicable* indicators to stakeholders.

I previously introduced you to a customizable principle of *The Business Puzzle Method*™ approach that I call PERPETUAL PROSPECTING. This is how your business collects, processes and utilizes information and data to advance INSIGHT, UNDERSTANDING and FORESIGHT. Durable customer and marketplace needs for today and in the future. This is how you create durable value.

PERPETUAL PROSPECTING is a practice of keeping current (relevant and resilient) with changing customer expectations, real-time customer experiences and industry / marketplace developments. Some strategies deployed are as follows:

Amazon focused on customer experiences as the key to creating a strategic advantage…based on convenience, price and selection.

As an M&A transactional specialist, these were criteria I reviewed to determine business viability and to negotiate business valuation. I call this *Business Plan Assumption Validation* (BPAV). All forward-looking businesses plans are based on forecasted assumptions. These assumptions are someone's best guess. *Perpetual Planning* and *Continuous Improvement* strategic conclusions need to be substantiated via such things as test market results, clinical trials, peer group assessments, surveys, and focus groups as applicable for your industry. I find that knowledge can also be obtained from competitive public company 10ks (reports filed by public companies with the U.S. Securities Exchange Commission) and consulting company assessments.

Forecasted assumptions need to be frequently validated to demonstrate that your business's vision for your business model is not just a romanticized notion.

Risk reduction is about proving that your company is best suited to solve a specific customer problem; Untested strategic plans, invalidated operational processes and unsubstantiated market need will attract little stakeholder interest.

Planning and raising capital are ongoing activities for a CEO and the C-suite leaders. A company will need funding to meet requirements for every stage of growth. Hopefully a company will be receiving ample revenue to fund most scaling requirements and be producing ample cash inflows. If not, a company will need multiple rounds of investor money to meet plan requirements. In addition, a company should be constantly evaluating performance of strategic plans in the marketplace to determine if its business model is working to the highest degree possible. *The Business Puzzle Method*™ should be constantly reviewed and implemented to decide when and if it is time for strategic changes and/or time to branch out into other target markets.

Operating a profitable, scalable high-growth business requires a constant scan of customer needs/wants, competitive actions, resource interactions, and industry ecosystem/environmental developments. Utilizing The *Business Puzzle Method*™ will allow a company to continually evaluate the success of a Business Model Statement and help develop alternate paths needed to launch updates as necessary.

Viewing the "fit" requirements to satisfy customers and the requirements from the investor community at large, generally the same analysis principles are needed to commercialize and/or are needed to grow a business, from a project analysis and presentation perspective. For this reason, I combined growth/scaling analysis needs with analysis needs for fund raising activities in the *Raising Capital* section of this book. In either case, validate program growth rationale before going-to-market.

Avoid spending extensive product/service resources until the Business Model Statement is supported by a completed risk mitigation and funds flow assessment.

This should be accomplished by performing a *Feasibility Analysis (FA)* as part of your business's decision-making process as a way to prioritize plans and determine business benefits and financial returns.

Successful business development requires the integration of necessary components at the right time and in the proper quantities.

Think of a durable business development program as sort of like baking a loaf of bread. You need the right mix of ingredients blended in the appropriate manner and baked for the correct length of time...to make a predictable outcome.

So often I have seen well intended CEOs build a product (an app for instance) and then begin spending large amounts of money on additional development, without validation. I recommend that you validate things such as:

- Extent of market demand.
- Price to charge customers.
- Cost to produce, deliver and service.
- People and technology resource requirements.
- Additional development anticipated to satisfy requirements for today and tomorrow.
- Funding requirements for all stages of lifecycle growth.

There are many reasons why business models fail or succeed. By following ongoing business development practices (as included in *The*

Business Puzzle Method™ approach) it is possible to evaluate, prioritize strategies and increase confidence in business development plan (s) feasibility.

A well-organized founder and/or CEO and C-suite leadership team of an established company needs to be skilled at strategic planning, allocating task activities and obtaining necessary funding in a timely manner. By implementing the relevant portions of *The Business Puzzle Method*™ approach as an operational best practice, a company will be able to plan and execute strategically and tactically to increase its ability to achieve milestones for both short-term and long-term sustainable, profitable, growth.

The Business Puzzle Method™ Foundation Practices

(Where Business Development Planning Meets Results)

This is a book about achieving and maintaining *Resilient* and *Durable Business Model* success through *Business Development* enabling practices that cover such aspects as governance, marketing/sales, human capital know-how, brand building, risk management and the breaking down of barriers for growth. It is based on my diversified experiences and learnings about how businesses can meet challenges and pursue growth strategies.

Dreams, desire and ambition alone will not make for a successful business. You need to devise strategies, tactics and plans (to include programs of execution) that are unique to your business purpose of achieving and maintaining profitable year-over-year sustainable value, as a growth business. There are no shortcuts.

Business strength and success of highly successful businesses (of all sizes) typically follow a master plan of action, a concept which I have drawn upon and combined with my own personal experiences. The end goal is *resiliency* and *durability*.

WHY I CALL IT A PUZZLE

Business Development success requires identification, assembly and implementation of multiple combinations of piece parts (like in a jigsaw puzzle) to create and maintain a year-over-year durable business. This requires adopting timely strategies and plans of execution to align and implement the piece parts...an ongoing business development task to be *relevant, resilient* and *durable.*

Unfortunately, when developing a strategic business formation plan, you cannot follow the picture on the top of the box as you would do in putting a jigsaw puzzle together. Jigsaw puzzles are games with a previously defined end product that is easily seen. Business development formation plans are not.

A *Business Development formation plan* can also be puzzling, but it does not have a preconceived end product that can be easily seen before you even start assembling the puzzle. A successful business has to identify, evaluate and assemble the interlocking pieces to create the desired end product...a *durable* business with a *durable competitive advantage.* The parts aren't easily obtained just by opening a jigsaw puzzle box. However, when *The Business Puzzle Method*™ approach is followed, your business will ultimately produce a justifiable *synergistic path* to follow...complete with interlocking short-term and longer-term piece parts.

Just-in-Time Transition Planning (JITTP)

Numerous factors affect the path to **durability**. Some are more influential than others depending on your industry of operation. In any case, the underlying rationale of strategies and tactics need to be constantly scrutinized to be **relevant, resilient** and **durable** in good times and bad. What is needed are business model (s) with year-over-year validated growth potential. I recommend a business development method I call **Just-in-Time Transition Planning (JITTP).**

The Underlying Principles

One strength by itself does not make for a long-term successful business... interrelated and interdependent unified parts working together make a business successful.

The underlying principle of *The Business Puzzle Method*™ approach is what I call *Just-In-Time Transition Planning (JITTP).* It is a way of dealing with change, challenges, opportunities and expansion plans... developed from multiple collaborative business-decision sources and perspectives. Following this practice will serve to maintain and grow overall business, business model and product / service *lifecycle longevity*.

Not all ideas can be developed into a successful business model. Innovation by itself does not guarantee that it will someday produce a viable program. What is needed is an evaluation process that combines *Perpetual Planning* activities with *Continuous Improvement* (of core capabilities) initiatives to determine strategic direction. This brings a wider scope into your decision-making process. Added benefits will be the increased ability to justify business plans while being perceived as risk-free as possible.

* * *

Adding to Insight, Understanding and Foresight

No business will ever have all the information desired to make decisions...however, you can focus on continually collecting, evaluating and prioritizing insight, understanding and related knowledge in a synergistic way to simplify directional prioritization of strategies and tactics and build trust in conclusions presented. This is part of what I call *Just-In-Time Transition Planning (JITTP)*. Practicing *Just-In-Time Transition Planning (JITTP)* is a great way to create business plan flexible options and prepare and execute to achieve desired outcomes and future plans.

To sum up *JITTP*...it is a business development practice to continually produce relevant insight and knowledge applicable for the satisfaction of the vision, mission, goals and the purpose of your business.

The Dimensions of Just-In-Time Transition Planning (JITTP)

JITTP is a business development initiative covering how to reach and maintain durability. It is a technique that includes identification, analysis and screening steps.

Three Actionable Baseline Requirements

Practicing ***Perpetual Planning*** and ***Continuous Improvement*** of core business practices and capabilities is a way to be constantly prepared to follow ***Growth Trajectories*** needed to avoid what I call **Strategic Complacency** (SC) often caused by following legacy business models as a status quo strategic solution. In addition, Perpetual Planning will help build a path to implement ***Seamless Continuity*** as needed to migrate between short-term and longer-term marketplace strategies.

- Perpetual Planning.
- Continuous Improvement of core business practices and capabilities.
- Tactical Execution.

Components for success

Before a business can be considered as a lifecycle durable business, it must demonstrate that it is relevant for both today and tomorrow's world. It must next also demonstrate that it can respond positively to disruptions, challenges and interruptions while addressing opportunities and everyday business requirements. I describe this as adapting to an ever-changing learning curve. Successful progress will lead your business to durability…and resulting profitable recurring growth.

- Relevancy
- Resiliency
- Durability

* * *

THE FOUR FUNDAMENTAL LEVELS OF PREPARATION

Successful business development should be an iterative, synchronized process. Following the **Four Levels** of plan preparation will help your business be ***Always-Ready*** and ***Performance Predictable…****which are imperatives to* set your business and business model (s) apart from your competition and to add value.

1. The Strategic Planning Phase

The first level should deal with the strategic implications covering the vision, mission, goals and purpose of your business plus the interrelationship of resources...design strategic intent, employee capabilities and requirements, financial and budgeting. It should be reflected in a business plan as:

- Business migration master plans.
- Continuous improvement initiatives.
- Contingency plans of action.

2. The Proof-of-Concept Verification Phase

The second level should deal with validation of assumptions driving strategies and tactics...feasibility analysis, customer requirements and preferences verification, marketplace size and growth rates, competitive assessment. It is what I call 360 degrees of evaluation.

3. The Operational Preparedness / Resource Readiness Phase

The third level should deal with anticipating and ensuring that operational requirements are in place utilizing insight, understanding and capabilities to focus resources...people resources, technology, servicing requirements, promotion programs, training requirements.

4. The Tactical Programs of Execution Phase

The fourth level should deal with plan execution following the strategies established and validated in the previous phases...Go-To-Market tactics, tactical plan timelines, marketing and sales activities, pivoting implementation requirements.

The Four Level Approach to Business Development

- Strategic planning (actionable, feasible and timely).
- Proof-of-Concept verification (360 degrees of evaluation).
- Operational preparedness (resource readiness).
- Tactical programs of execution (plan execution with a purpose).

Six Key Foundation Interdependencies Required

Planning to ultimately succeed in the long run requires a powerful synergistic method featuring clear and proactive requirements, innovative workflows and the capability to make strategies and tactics happen. This approach will allow for the development of a relevant and resilient transformation *Blueprint* to reach and maintain a durable business. In addition, it will give your business the ability to know when to make Strategic Redirection (pivoting) decisions and / or release new and improved as well as disruptive business models. *The Business Puzzle Method*™ approach addresses transformative influences...inside and outside of your business...imperative for business durable success.

Requirement #1 *Following a SYNERGISTIC ACTIONABLE PERPETUAL PLANNING PROCESS (SAPPP).*

Participation in real-time continuous planning to ensure relevant, timely and flexible tactical plan execution.

Requirement #2 *Embracing a BALANCED BUSINESS MIGRATION APPROACH (BBMA).*

Ensure continuity for seamless progression of business strategic direction from short-term to longer-term timeframes.

Requirement #3 *Operating in a PERPETUAL RESET MODE (PRM).*

Operating a business recognizing the need for continual operational, strategic and tactical expansion and updating.

Requirement #4 *Evaluating and updating via a BUSINESS MODEL REJUVENATION PROGRAM (BMRP).*

Recognizing that businesses and business models naturally go through lifecycle stages of growth and decline requiring continual updating.

Requirement #5 *Following a CUSTOMER and MARKETPLACE EXPANSION PROCESS (CMEP) .*

Actively prospecting for customers and markets that match relevant strategic-fit criteria in addition to revenue generation activities.

Requirement #6 *Preparation of compelling and defensible EVIDENCE-BASED SUBSTANTIATION (EBS).*

Be able to present justifiable, compelling strategic and tactical rationale that is poised for durability.

REQUIRED COMPONENTS DRIVING BUSINESS DEVELOPMENT SUCCESS

At this time, let us introduce the concept of being competitive by operating with **Balanced Future-Oriented programs** as fundamentals for *Perpetual Planning*. They need to be synergistic creating a collaborative decision-making culture capable of meeting customer demands and stakeholder (e.g. employees, funding sources, investors, partnerships, and advisors) requirements for today and in the future.

Eight Balanced Future-Oriented Program Components to be Lifecycle Durable:

Master Plans: to identify strategic and tactical transition options for consideration.

Ensure prioritization of relevant, resilient & durable customer-centric solutions.

- **Always-Ready:** to address changes, challenges and opportunities.

  Ensure timely response to customer and marketplace evolving needs.

- **Performance Predictable**: to convince audiences of capabilities and results.

  Ensure substantiation and validation of strategic and tactical rationale.

- **Continual Prospecting**: to have relevant insight, understanding and foresight.

Ensure data / information input for decision-making is current and factual.

- **Innovative Culture Alignment:** to encourage creativity and competitiveness.

Ensure human resources and business intent are aligned.

- **Seamless Strategies**: to combine short-term and longer-term considerations.

Ensure future business continuity.

- **Strong Brand Reputation:** to attract and retain the desired customer base.

Ensure customer loyalty stimulating new and repeat business.

- **Risk Management:** to increase confidence in dealing with uncertainty.

Ensure adequate contingency plans as courses of action.

- **Strategic and Tactical Substantiation:** to justify strategic and tactical rationale.

Ensure comprehension and belief in business purpose, vision, mission and goals.

An additional note - these eight future-oriented program components (when taken as aggregate facts) will strengthen the rationale justifying strategies and tactics and create higher value perceptions needed to strengthen a business's position during negotiation of various terms and conditions (T&C) discussion. This capability of increasing negotiating power as creates a significant *Competitive Advantage.*

Lifecycle Durability is very much dependent on the positioning strength of business Terms & Conditions negotiated during the lifecycle of a business.

These components are often missed, individually or in total. *The Business Puzzle Method*™ approach *brings* them together as a function of actionable *Perpetual Planning* practices.

For strategies and tactics to be successful, they must make sense across many interconnected categories of influence (e.g. C-suite, boards, marketing, manufacturing, supply chains, product management, customer support, and sales teams – all employees and support teams).

Chapter 8: The Business Puzzle Method ™

11 Puzzle Piece Principles

(An Applied Business Development Solution For Lifecycle Business Durability)

It takes a workforce with a Durability Focused Mindset (DFM) to produce relevant insight, knowledge and awareness needed to build and maintain durable transition plans of action.

The focus of the *11 Puzzle Piece Principles are core* tenets to preparing (and executing) what I call *Impactful Transition Plans* (ITP)...responsive to an ever-changing world of challenges, interruptions and opportunities. Rapidly expanding businesses drive change, not just react to landscape changes and competitive pressures.

Earlier in this book I discussed the *Just-In-Time Transition Planning (JITTP)* steps (as part of *The Business Puzzle Method*™ approach) that I described as the *Four Levels of Preparation...*as stages of planning and implementation.

As a reminder:

STAGES OF PLANNING / IMPLEMENTATION TO BE LIFCYCLE DURABLE

1. Strategic planning...*turn an idea into a successful and responsible business model.*

   Define what, where, how, who and when.

2. Proof-of-Concept verification...continuous 360 degrees of evaluation.

   Find markets, customer / marketplace need and go-to-market approach.

3. Operational preparedness...*be resource ready.*

   People requirements, operational resources, capabilities, financial needs.

4. Tactical programs of execution...*prepare to launch, grow & be profitable.*

   Implement Go-to-Market actions, advertising & promotion, tracking & measurement.

SUPPORTING THE FOUR PLANNING / IMPLEMENTATION STAGES

Consider the four planning / implementation stages of *The Business Puzzle Method*™ approach as a *pre-planning* and *rejuvenation process* to keep your business connected to the real world. It is most effective when performed as a perpetual / ongoing information collection, evaluation and execution activity. This approach fits our world that never stops changing, either by design or otherwise. Following *The Business Puzzle Method*™ *11 Puzzle Piece Principles* is what it takes for:

- *Perpetual Planning*: to identify, design and operate year-over-year *durable* business models.

- *Continuous Improvement:* to identify, design and operate with solutions needed to close performance gaps.

- *Tactical Execution*: to implement actionable, successful real-time operations and marketplace engagements.

The Business Puzzle Method™ *11 Puzzle Piece Principles* address multiple aspects (a best lineup of real-world variants) that can be tailored to your industry. Following the *11 Puzzle Piece Principles* will make your business more predictable, substantiates valuation and will be perceived as less risky.

Successful vision driven goal achievement and outcomes are easier to achieve when you have the right data/information, people resources, culture, and tools to assist you.

WHAT IT IS

The Business Puzzle Method™ approach, with the *11 Puzzle Piece Principles,* will help your business development and maintain a versatile playbook (demonstrating business evolution, new growth solutions and profits) to build and operate transformative strategic and tactical *relevant, resilient, durable and predictable performance outcomes.*

Today, Business Development needs to be an iterative process of overlapping / supportive influencing points creating insight, foresight and successful durable outcomes.

The role of *continual lifecycle business development* is now more important than ever. It requires plans and goals for *durability* to be a paramount priority while functioning in day-to-day activities in this current and future business world. This requires understanding what I have identified as a *cluster of dependencies*...leading to managing, maintaining and continually reconstructing strategies, tactics and business models to drive durable growth and profitability.

Lifecycle Durability requires aligning the many influences that will create and maintain a Competitive Advantage.

This section of the book, *"The Quest for Durability,"* deals with the *11 Puzzle Piece Principles* to be followed to deal with what I call the *New*

Reality (the future), as previously discussed in earlier chapters. Together, the *11 Puzzle Piece Principles* create a justifiable, documented story substantiating a *Durable Competitive Advantage.* Insights obtained from the collective knowledge contained from the *11 Puzzle Piece Principles* of *The Business Puzzle Method*™ approach will remove barriers (internal and external to your business) to reach and maintain year-over-year long-term *durability.*

THE THREE CENTERING GOALS

Following the *11 Puzzle Piece Principles* of *The Business Puzzle Method*™ approach will be enormously helpful in keeping your business focused on what I call the three *Centering Goals* (CG) of business development planning and execution...by being *centered* on – *Purpose, Progress* and *Perpetuality.* They collectively define expectations, growth paths for your business's destiny and need to be understood at all levels of your business.

DEFINING PURPOSE, PROGRESS and PERPETUALITY

Framing Business Development activities needed to be centered on Purpose, Progress and Perpetuality to produce justifiable business decisions and successful actions.

As previously discussed, *The Business Puzzle Method*™ approach (with supporting principles) features a systematic and rational aligning process that I call *Business Centering (BC).* I define the practice of Centering Business Development as continually focusing and constantly updating the three Ps...a "big picture" definition.

#1: Purpose: Communicating a business's purpose throughout a business organization has a tremendous unifying influence. Leadership teams, employees and support organizations need to be engaged and focused on the same values and goals. This is alignment of current and future reasons a business entity exists. Going forward, customer buying preferences will be increasingly influenced by the perception of such things as environment and social impacts...it will more and more be a part of what people consider as defining a responsible business.

Being able to consistently understand (customers, funding sources, partners, and employees) a business's *purpose* adds an important *Competitive Advantage* driving effective group (organization-wide) dynamics.

In addition, customer buying preferences are highly influenced by their understanding of what a business stands for (its purpose), beyond delivering profits. This is a perspective influencing business, business models and product / service lifecycles.

Purpose Perception (PP) is a driver of behavioral actions, which could be either good or bad. A unified *purpose* makes sport teams successful. Everybody on the team understands the *purpose* of their contribution to generate successful outcomes—a concept also true for fast growing businesses. Concerns for such things as a business's impact on environmental and social change need to be part of a business's *purpose* considerations since customer perceptions around these matters impacts sales, customer loyalty, and can instill or damage brand trust.

The Walt Disney Company has a mission statement that clearly demonstrates their purpose:

"The mission of The Walt Disney Company is to entertain, inform and inspire people around the globe through the power of unparalleled storytelling, reflecting the iconic brands, creative minds and innovative technologies that make ours the world's premier entertainment company."

Lifecycle durability requires clear communication of business purpose and adherence to the mission statement. Following the perception of their business purpose and mission statement has made them arguably a great entertainment company!

#2: Progress: Business entities that stay too long in their legacy business models soon start to lose market share and some have experienced bankruptcy. Businesses that continually expand their scope, update business models and market approach / solutions grow to remain viable businesses.

RadioShack, formerly RadioShack Corporation, was a retailer founded in 1921. In **February 2015**, RadioShack (RSHCQ), a renowned electronics store, filed for Chapter 11 bankruptcy protection following many financial and operational missteps. Basically, RadioShack missed the movement to online sales and by failing to stock stores with relevant items for purchase. This occurred even though they were one of the earliest retailers to manufacture and sell home computers (TRS-80) and TVs. Their inability to plan for the future eventually made them irrelevant in the marketplace.

Sears went from the largest retailer in the world to bankruptcy
Some of their brands are still well known in the business world today:

- Allstate Insurance
- Craftsman Tools
- Kenmore Appliances
- DieHard Batteries

Interesting, Sears's product and service brand appeal was worth more than the Sears business itself. In addition, Sears had its beginnings in the mail-order catalogue business which could be viewed as the origin of the concept for e-commerce sales.

The story around the diminished appeal of these two businesses could be a book in itself. Simply stated, to sum up, their demise was an obsession with the past as reflected in *strategic complacency* which made their stores less than relevant. Their current customer world changed (growing competitive stores, a declining interest in catalog sales and growing preferences for e-commerce) —but they did not change.

As I emphasize via *The Business Puzzle Method*™ approach explanations, progress constantly needs reevaluating core capabilities, tracking and reacting to change, performing interruptions and constantly addressing opportunities. Progress (accomplishments and plans) need to be clearly delineated on *Milestone* charts and within financial reviews.

#3: Perpetuality: Year-over-year and long-term lifecycle *durability* must be achieved by following a methodology that leads to *continuance* from short-term to long-term profitable growth...as is possible by following *The Business Puzzle Method*™ approach. Business development does not stop with planning, it must include execution.

I call this *Business Development Perpetuality (BDP)...*which I define as business positioning which does not have an end date. Outcomes are derived from a stream of synergistic strategic and tactical (executable) transformation plans focused on being a year-over-year *relevant, resilient, durable* business entity.

You should consider *Business Development Perpetuality (BDP) as the end goal of any business looking to be a lifecycle value creating, durable business. Business Development Perpetuality (BDP)* is best explained as developing and implementing preconceived programs rationalizing year-over-year business CONTINUITY. Not CONTINUITY just from a disaster recover perspective but from actionable *Perpetual Planning* and *Continuous Improvement* initiatives. The *Quest for Durability / The Business Puzzle Method*™ approach has the framework to organize and develop timely, flexible options for multiple lifecycle durability strategies and tactics needed to address CONTINUITY...year-over-year transition requirements.

Businesses that demonstrate Perpetuality are the favorite companies of investors in the stock market. To be "fundable" they continually reinvent their business models to demonstrate relevancy, resilience and durability.

A LOOK AT THE 11 PUZZLE PIECE PRINCIPLES

Consider the *11 Puzzle Piece Principles* as an adrenaline-packed summarization of the essential requirements really needed for a business to create and maintain enduring executable *durability*. Following the *11Puzzle Piece Principles*, will enhance confidence so that your business can take on the changing world head-on in a synergistic, justifiable fashion. It represents my A-List of actions that will drive desirability in your business...from customers, developers, funding sources, partners as well as employees.

* * *

THE 11 PUZZLE PIECE PRINCIPLES OF *The Business Puzzle Method*™ APPROACH

Following the *11 Puzzle Piece Principles of The Business Puzzle Method*™ approach will assist your business in determining which blueprints to build and which paths to follow to be a year-over-year durable business.

Information prospecting, screening, analyzing and prioritizing are fundamental requirements for any business to be relevant, resilient and durable over time. The ideas identified in the following *11 Puzzle Piece Principles* are intended to be thought provokers, based on experiences I observed throughout my career. The *11 Puzzle Piece Principles* should be considered foundational to the development of your business's transformational evolution strategies and tactical execution plans as your business vies for an ongoing dominant competitive advantage in chosen marketplaces. They need to be completed (and continuously updated) to reflect your business's specific mission, plans and goals.

THE 11 PUZZLE PIECE PRINCIPLES DEFINED

The 11 Puzzle Piece Principles provide a basis to substantiate the rationale for transformative strategies and tactics.

I designed the *11 Puzzle Piece Principles* (each with multidimensional purpose) to help increase the insight and effectiveness of your business's strategic and tactical transformation programs. Effectiveness is dependent on many vital factors such as: people, team chemistry, communication practices, performance measurement parameters, brand reputation, training, culture, and servicing capabilities. They require collaboration and business-specific decision-making for your business to be a year-over-year *relevant, resilient* and *durable* business entity.

The *11 Puzzle Piece Principles* must be synergistically connected in order to maximize their impact. In a given situation, some of the *11 Puzzle Piece Rules* may be more synergistic than others given specific industries, fit criteria, commercial value and prioritization of strategic intent. It should not be considered a rigid approach.

Let's look into this further...as they pertain to your business.

APPLYING THE 11 PUZZLE PIECE PRINCIPLES

One of the main benefits of following **The Business Puzzle Method™** ***approach for lifecycle longevity business development is that you will be employing a process focused on obtaining a future vision to make your business's future more certain and to be viewed as a durable reality.***

Advanced planning with actionable implementation programs is a powerful business development approach to achieve and maintain continuous durability and a competitive advantage. Following the *11 Puzzle Piece Principles* will keep your business's strategies and tactics constantly refreshed.

Completing *The Business Puzzle Method*™ *11 Puzzle Piece Principles* for your business will amplify strengths to increase comprehension of your business's capabilities, reduce perceived risk and increase bargaining power.

To me, the *11 Puzzle Piece Principles* are *durability essentials*. They demonstrate an appealing ability to operate effectively to improve, enhance and grow a business or a business unit within a business.

Keeping the 11 Puzzle Piece Principles current adds to your business strength by collectively adding insight and understanding to explanations of your business's growth transition plans.

* * *

Addressing Resources, Capabilities & Needs for Business Development

It is important to continually update insight, knowledge, understanding and strategic decisions.

Status-quo is not a sufficient strategy for durability.

It is no secret that the quest for business durability has become more complex and therefore in need of well thought-out and timely transition strategies and corresponding execution of tactical plans. Hence the origin of the title and theme of this book.

To accomplish this, I suggest adding an ongoing cross-functional *business development* capability to your operational activities. Success today and in the future revolves around the capability to understand marketplace and landscape realities, making justifiable decisions and acting accordingly in a timely manner. This should not be done in a fragmented way and should never be an afterthought.

Durable business development should be a team event adding insight, knowledge, and foresight thus creating value and achieving and maintaining profitable growth objectives.

Dealing with the pearls of reality within your business, among and between associates and partners and in the marketplace is a full-time activity. The degree of success depends on creating a cultural environment of collaborative belief in purpose, vision, mission, goals and capabilities...driven by the principles of *Perpetual Planning* and *Continuous Improvement* of core capabilities.

I call this practice creating a *Business Development Infrastructure Capability* (BDIC).

The 11 Puzzle Piece Principles will make it possible for business plans (and supporting plans) to be more comprehensible and believable. It is a great way to ensure strategies, tactics and capabilities are a fit with business purpose, vision, mission and goals. In addition, preplanning to possess the *11 Puzzle Piece Principles* (that are relevant for your business) will make closing growth discussions and marketplace positioning easier and more timely.

This approach will help your business always be ready to address intentional and unintentional emerging business and marketplace influences...with flexible, speedy time-to-market substantiated solutions!

The 11 Business Puzzle Principles will serve as both a short-term and long-term approach to achieve and maintain year-over-year durability and value-added.

Define the 11 Puzzle Piece Principles Specifically for Your Business

Following the 11 Puzzle Piece Principles will guide your business to create and substantiate a blueprint and growth path for your business to be a year-over-year relevant, resilient and durable success.

Following the 11 Puzzle Piece Principles will serve as a durability reinforcing discipline.

Business development, to future-proof your business, is not a sedentary process.

These *11 Puzzle Piece Principles* represent an "a la carte" program to help you define, explain and substantiate your business's strategic direction. It addresses the fundamental ingredients (the nuts and bolts) needed to make your business durable.

The *11 Puzzle Piece Principles* should be viewed as *Actionable Synergies (AS)*, addressing durability as a perpetual *Business Development* problem... helping your business find and implement the best fit for strategic transition and tactical execution. View them as reinforcing elements keeping your business moving forward and not being stalled by complacency or indecision.

Business success is achieved by continually concentrating on being durability fit (DF).

Just as being durably fit (physical conditioning) is critical for athletics, being durability fit is critical for your business's performance success, growth and survival. Physical fitness conditioning includes strengthening exercises and constant workouts to test capabilities to enhance capabilities. This concept of being *durability fit (DF)* is embedded as a foundation principle driving the *11 Puzzle Piece Principles* for business durability.

Personalize your definition (from business mission perspective) of being *Durability Fit (DF)*. Consider each of the *11 Puzzle Piece Principles* in the context of various stages of your overall business / industry, business model and product / service *lifecycle longevity*. *Lifecycle* stages (from marketplace introduction through maturity) often have different requirements to remain viable. Draw on *Perpetual Planning learnings* and *Continuous Improvement initiatives* to proactively update insight, knowledge and foresight...especially as they pertain to the *11 Puzzle Piece Principles*.

Adopt the habit of elaborating and frequently updating them (as needed to define growth specifically for your business and industry). In so doing, your business should leave the perceived relative safety of the land of status quo and participate in the untested growing world of the future. Highly successful businesses typically follow this philosophy for business growth. Unicorn businesses (privately held startup businesses with a value of over $1 billion) clearly build on their original legacy business models (i.e. Apple, Uber, Airbnb, Space X).

The 11 Puzzle Piece Principles will serve as a creative guideline to develop a path leading to successful durable business transformation.

Adopting The 11 Puzzle Piece Principles as a business development practice will allow for an increase in insight, understanding and foresight...important ingredients for performance excellence and operating as a durable business entity.

The Path to Lifecycle Continuity, Durability and Value Creation

The 11 Puzzle Piece Principles encapsulates the fundamentals inherent in The Business Puzzle Method™ *approach to help make plans more executable and more likely to be predictable and successful with a focus on agility, timing, relevancy and business lifecycle durability.*

Puzzle Piece Principle #1 – ***Agile Management Philosophy***
(Focus on harmonizing mission, strategy, culture, governance and decision-making.)

> ***Principle #1:*** Always operate and develop your business with the objective of achieving predictable short-term and longer-term year-over-year continuity.
>
> > ***Principle #1 Comment:*** Durability happens when you follow business purpose, vision, mission and goals beyond just short-term objectives.

Puzzle Piece Principle #2 – ***Agile, Flexible Team Interactions and Collaborative Support***
(Building collective alignment & mindset to enable achievement of business goals.)

> ***Principle #2:*** Always draw upon insight from people from all parts of your business's (internal and external) infrastructure in strategic and tactical decision-making.
>
> > ***Principle #2 Comment:*** Durability happens when you utilize the collective learnings drawn from within collaborative cultures, leadership and team cooperation, and relevant / timely customer and marketplace knowledge sources.

Puzzle Piece Principle #3 – *Business Feasibility and Value Creation*
(Assessing potential opportunities.)

> ***Principle # 3:*** Always test, evaluate and understand strategic and financial outcome feasibility anticipated for existing and transitional strategic and tactical actions.
>
> > **Principle # 3 Comment:** Durability is best justified when a pipeline of strategic and tactical options has been assessed to be feasible and prioritized for implementation.

Puzzle Piece Principle #4 – Prepare for *Business Model Development, Validation and Readiness for Adjustments*
(Focus on customer satisfaction, readiness, timeliness, growth and continuity.)

> ***Principle # 4:*** Always be aware of business model (s) and product / service lifecycle longevity as measured by customer / marketplace acceptance.
>
> > **Principle #4 Comment**: Durability is about having year-over-year relevant, resilient and successful marketplace adoption.

Puzzle Piece Principle #5 – Prepare Milestones and Progress Reports
(Conveying critical steps, dependencies, targeted outcomes and traction measurement.)

> ***Principle #5:*** Always be willing to communicate business points of progress and anticipated future steps.
>
> > ***Principle #5 Comment:*** Durability comprehension requires that stakeholders monitor and understand key tangible accomplishment, dependencies and forward-looking checkpoints.

Puzzle Piece Principle #6 – Prepare Market Plans and Tactical Execution Programs
(Being focused on marketplace, customer needs, solution delivery and brand reputation.)

> ***Principle #6:*** Always have market plans with marketing strategies and tactics that fit with business plan overall strategic intent business models producing great customer experiences… for today and for tomorrow.
>
>> ***Principle #6 Comment:*** Durability requires a continual go-to-market strategy to ensure brand acceptance and resilient business models (with relevant products and services) are constantly being delivered in the marketplace.

Puzzle Piece Principle #7 – Prepare Customer Engagement Practices and Touchpoint Utilization
(Continual prospecting to source insight, understanding, foresight while making sales)

> ***Principle #7:*** Always use multiple customer engagement practices (in the buyer journey) that best match continually evolving customer preferences in target markets.
>
>> ***Principle #7 Comment:*** Durability requires keeping up with current and changing customer engagement practices applicable for growth programs and changing marketplace evolution.

Puzzle Piece Principle #8 – Prepare Business Plans and Linked Operational Plans
(Proactively develop, and present strategies, tactics and market tested customer solutions.)

***Principle** #8*: Always have a document (s) that synergistically and logically explains strategic plans, identifies resource requirements and tactical plans of execution.

> ***Principle #8 Comment:*** Durability requires a document (a blueprint) and a roadmap defining linked transitional strategic plans and tactical programs of execution to be prioritized and implemented over various time periods.

Puzzle Piece Principle #9 – Prepare Financial Statements, Department Contribution, Environmental, Social and Governance (ESG) Reports

(Building, presenting and explaining quality of earnings performance and how functional organizational and durable investing programs are contributing.)

***Principle** # 9:* Always be able to explain a historical and forward-looking rationale for the earning power and cash flow impacts of your business plans for a mix of possible funding sources.

> ***Principle #9 Comment:*** Durability requires being able to demonstrate evidence-based rationale and financial substantiation (financial legitimacy) of strategies, tactics and valuations as measured as top-line revenue growth, bottom-line earnings growth and return on invested capital.

Puzzle Piece Principle #10 –Prepare Risk Management and Risk Avoidance Assessments

(Neutralizing the fear of risk and uncertainty)

Principle #10: Always reduce uncertainty perceptions about strategic and tactical plans and initiatives while operating within a calculated chosen level of risk tolerance.

Principle #10 Comment: Durability requires producing mitigating measures in the form of contingency plans, strategic redirection (pivoting) plans, and growth options to reduce concerns for uncertainty.

Puzzle Piece Principle #11 – Prepare Due Diligence Assessment Readiness Materials

(Satisfying the need for readily accessible requisite disclosures)

***Principle** #11:* Always be prepared to present key basic information needed for growth situations (partnerships, M&A, Joint Ventures, divestment) investigations and audits.

***Principle** #11 **Comment**:* Durability often requires preemptive work completed to support prescreening / vetting processes to shorten evaluation timelines, speed the steps to closures and demonstrate the willingness to negotiate.

APPENDIX

About Cultivating Durable Foundational Best Practices

Amid a marketplace of continual turbulence, change and unending fields of opportunities, there are ground rules that lead to business lifecycle longevity and durability...the Ten Rs of Durability.

As was emphasized throughout this book, for a business to have a durable lifecycle it has to be in a continuous mode of transformation. Realities are constantly shifting as the world changes and evolves around us. However, I did identify 10 criteria I consider constants, regardless of the strategic direction and tactical execution programs your business follows.

Business success is a complex undertaking. To improve success rates, I have identified high-level common characteristics that give a business a performance edge. I named them the *10 Rs of Durability*. I consider them as *Durability Goals (DG)*, relevant for any business, in any stage of growth and in any industry. When addressed as part of a goal creating process, they stimulate confidence and durable performance predictability.

They represent a type of baseline checklist, which when achieved will create believable long-term value for your business. I consider them as *Durability Performance Objectives (DPO)*. Meeting these objectives is no easy task. Following The *Business Puzzle Method*™ approach will expedite development of transitional links for strategic plans and programs of tactical execution, to help your business get there. Output from *The Business Puzzle Method*™ approach will produce the evidence your business will need to achieve, maintain and communicate points emphasizing lifecycle durability.

Note: The *10 Rs for Durability* are applicable for total businesses, divisions or business units of businesses in all phases of lifecycle growth!

The 10 Rs to Keep Your Eye on the Goal of Lifecycle Durability

Relevant – be compatible with customer value propositions and marketplace wants, needs and preferences.

Resilient – enable year-over-year perpetual planning and continuous improvement of core capabilities.

Readiness – prepare validated & prioritized business model migration plans & execution tactics.

Rejuvenate – be willing to change legacy / status quo strategic decisions as needed to advance business and business model longevity.

Rationale – have defensible business model (s) linked with actionable business, operational, and financial plans.

Real-Time – perform continual prospecting for current and anticipated business insight, understanding and opportunities.

Resources – have a timely, flexible collaborative aligned mix of knowledgeable human capital, technology, assets, financial capabilities, & support services.

Reengineering – close major strategic and tactical gaps and address new opportunities through newly envisioned operational and marketplace solutions.

Reputation – maintain perceived high regard in the opinion of industry influencers, customers and other stakeholders.

Risk-Reduction – emphasize risk assessment alternative strategies & contingency plans to reduce concerns for uncertainty.

Achieving and maintaining the rationale behind the *10 Rs of Durability* will protect and increase the long-term value and competitive advantage of your business. Continual assessments need to be part of your business's Perpetual Planning, Continuous Improvement Initiatives and Strategic and Tactical Execution to ensure that *The 10 Rs of Durability* are always relevant and defendable.

About the Author

Jerry Creighton, Sr., MBA is an award-winning entrepreneur, corporate executive, business owner, angel investor, adjunct lecturer, author, former army officer, and a practicing consultant. His experience includes the role of an examiner for the AT&T's Chairman's Quality Award program which adopted use of the Malcolm Baldrige National Quality criteria (the highest level of national recognition for performance excellence that a U.S. organization can receive).

Jerry takes an innovator's approach to business development. He is passionate about accelerating creative entrepreneurship, business and economic growth and job creation through the advancement of organizations and business entities. He has worked in multiple industries within 17 countries, working closely with businesses of all sizes to help them scale and implement year-over-year durable organizational excellence and growth commercialization transitions. Jerry's extensive business development experience spans business ownership and domestic USA and international executive positions with Xerox, AT&T, Lucent and Deutsche Telekom. They include mergers and acquisitions / joint ventures, market management, business planning, financial reporting, and business operations responsibilities.

In addition, Jerry served more than a decade as a past Executive Director of the iconic Enterprise Development Center (EDC)...renamed VentureLink...at New Jersey Institute of Technology (NJIT), arguably one of the most successful incubators and expansion company commercialization centers in New Jersey with typically over 90 resident and nonresident member companies (domestic USA and international) per year.

In his book *The Quest for Durability* Jerry chose the term *The Business Puzzle Method*™ approach as a metaphor to showcase the cross-disciplinary synergies required to identify, evaluate and move strategic plans and tactical execution actions from an idea to a justifiable opportunity, to a successful long-lasting business model... as needed to produce viable, profitable long-lasting organizations / businesses. It represents an effective and deliberate program to nurture and propel year-over-year relevant, resilient and durable organizations / businesses into the future. Jerry has a BA and an MBA from Widener University. Jerry also completed an Executive Program "Managing Negotiations "at Columbia University.

Thank you for reading.
Please review this book. Reviews
help others find Absolutely Amazing eBooks and
inspire us to keep providing these marvelous titles.
If you would like to be put on our email list
to receive updates on new releases,
contests, and promotions, please go to
AbsolutelyAmazingEbooks.com and sign up.

For sales, editorial information, subsidiary rights information
or a catalog, please write or phone or e-mail
AbsolutelyAmazingEbooks
Manhanset House
Shelter Island Hts., New York 11965-0342, US
Tel: 212-427-7139
www.AbsolutelyAmazingEbooks.com
bricktower@aol.com
www.IngramContent.com

For sales in the UK and Europe please contact our distributor,
Gazelle Book Services
White Cross Mills
Lancaster, LA1 4XS, UK
Tel: (01524) 68765 Fax: (01524) 63232
email: jacky@gazellebooks.co.uk

www.ingramcontent.com/pod-product-compliance
Lightning Source LLC
Chambersburg PA
CBHW060604210326
41519CB00014B/3561
9781955036481